April 1957. Don Hoak, third baseman for the Cincinnati Reds, makes one of baseball's historic fielding plays. He scoops up an easy grounder and tosses the ball to the shortstop for an easy out —on himself!

Hoak was a runner on second base and Gus Bell on first with one down when their Reds teammate Wally Post hit a soft grounder toward Braves shortstop Johnny Logan. Logan got set to start a double play.

But on his way from second base to third Hoak scooped up the ball with his bare hands, then flipped it to an astonished Logan.

WHAT HAPPENED TO HOAK, BELL AND POST? YOU BE THE UMPIRE!

Hoak broke up a potential double play by sacrificing himself. And he got away with it—slamming his historic gambit right through a loophole in the rule book. The rules state that when a runner is struck by a batted ball before a fielder has a chance to make a play, the base runner is automatically out—*and the batter is awarded first base.* Hoak was called out, but the Reds' rally remained alive. Bell advanced safely to second. The rules were later rewritten so that if a runner deliberately interferes with a batted ball to break up a double play, the ball is declared dead and both the runner and the batter are automatically out.

But on April 21, 1957, Wally Post was credited with a single—the only legitimate hit in baseball history to have been fielded by a player on the batter's own team!

Also by Richard Goldstein:

SPARTAN SEASONS:
How Baseball Survived the Second World War

SUPERSTARS AND SCREWBALLS:
100 Years of Brooklyn Baseball

YOU BE THE UMPIRE!

THE BASEBALL CONTROVERSY QUIZ BOOK

RICHARD GOLDSTEIN

A Dell Trade Paperback

FOR NANCY

Contents

Acknowledgments

I'm grateful to Mitch Horowitz of Dell for his insight and encouragement.

In recounting madcap moments, Eldon Auker, Clay Bryant, Billy Herman, Frank Saucier, George Selkirk and Monte Weaver shared their recollections with me.

The National League umpire and crew chief John McSherry was kind enough to clear up some deliciously confusing situations.

I appreciate the efforts of Stuart Krichevsky in ably representing me.

My wife, Nancy, was there as always with her loving support.

Preface

"No manager, player, substitute, coach, trainer or batboy shall at any time, whether from the bench, the coach's box or on the playing field, or elsewhere use language which will in any manner refer to or reflect upon opposing players, an umpire, or any spectator"—Regulation 4.06 (a) (2), "Official Playing Rules."

"It's a goddamn shame to lose a goddamn game because of that goddamn call"—Carlton Fisk.

On the afternoon of June 19, 1846, a group of young men clad in natty blue pantaloons, white flannel shirts and straw hats gathered in the community of

YOU BE THE UMPIRE!

Hoboken, New Jersey, with bat and ball in hand. They called themselves the Knickerbockers. Playing at the bucolic Elysian Fields, they matched their primitive skills against a squad known simply as the New York club. It was the first fully documented match game in the history of baseball.

The players prided themselves on being "gentlemen"—they were mainly businessmen, merchants and clerks. Yet by the time the afternoon had ended with a 23–1 victory for New York, the excitement of competition had gotten the best of good manners.

The umpire that day—Alexander Cartwright, the Knickerbockers' founder and baseball's rule-making pioneer—fined a New York ballplayer named James Whyte Davis half a York shilling for swearing.

That autumn, it was a member of the Knickerbockers who incurred an umpire's wrath for disorderly baseball conduct. Ebinezer Dupignac was fined, according to club records, "6 cents for saying s——t."

Baseball was in its infancy—the games supposedly nothing more than social occasions—but the arguing had begun.

By the 1880s, the game was a rowdy affair with hard-nosed ballplayers and managers confronting equally tough umpires. The ump was transformed into a caricature: an upholder of law and order whom everyone loved to hate.

A poem published in 1886 captured the umpire's image:

PREFACE

Mother, may I slug the umpire,
May I slug him right away?
So he cannot be here, Mother,
When the clubs begin to play?

      *   *   *

Let me climb his frame, dear Mother,
While the happy people shout;
I'll not kill him dearest Mother,
I will only knock him out.

But it went beyond ridicule by rhyme.

One afternoon in the mid-1880s, John Montgomery Ward of the New York Giants cut up Umpire John Gaffney's eye in a slugging match. The punishment: a fine but only a brief suspension, since Ward apologized and even took Gaffney to visit a surgeon. And Ward happened to be one of nineteenth-century baseball's more respectable characters. He'd attended Penn State and would go on to become a lawyer.

Sometimes the fans were even rougher than the players or managers. Umpire Tim Hurst was one day the target of a "crystal shower"—a barrage of beer mugs from the stands—in August 1897 at Cincinnati. Hurst was no Milquetoast. He threw one of the mugs back into the seats. It struck a fan, causing severe head injuries, and the ump was arrested on a charge of assault with intent to kill. He was convicted, but got off with a hundred-dollar fine.

Even the sportswriters joined in umpire-baiting,

YOU BE THE UMPIRE!

and here, too, the umps sometimes fought back. Al Jennings, an umpire of the 1880s, went to a Washington newspaper office to confront a reporter who had insulted him. But the ump met his match—the paper's sports editor pummeled him with a paste pot and tossed him out.

By the early twentieth century, umpires were being treated as professionals, and the abuse was toned down. (There were a few notable exceptions, like the day in 1906 when John McGraw ordered the gatekeepers to bar Umpire Jim Johnstone from the Polo Grounds.)

Today, the umpires are well paid, well trained and reasonably well respected. They even have an aggressive union, as Lou Piniella found out in the summer of 1991. The Cincinnati Reds' manager was hit with a $5-million defamation suit by the Major League Umpires Association after accusing Umpire Gary Darling of bias against his team.

Though the umps don't live in fear of their lives anymore, the pressure may be greater than ever. With instant replay, the TV tape machine subjects decisions made in a split second to scrutiny by millions of fans.

The umps seem to be right most of the time, but when they're not, the visual proof is there. Electronic Exhibit No. 1 is Don Denkinger's much-maligned "safe" call at first base on Jorge Orta that helped keep the Kansas City Royals alive in the 1985 World

PREFACE

Series they would eventually capture from the St. Louis Cardinals.

But the ump needs a lot more than a sharp pair of eyes. Under game pressure he must apply dozens of rules running to thousands of words. And beyond that there's the Case Book, material that elaborates on or interprets the rules.

Sometimes the rule book appears absurdly simple. Section 2.00 advises that "an infielder is a fielder who occupies a position in the infield." You have to go to umpiring school to learn that?

But things can get stickier.

Under the infield-fly rule, a batter is automatically out when he hits "a fair fly ball (not including a line drive nor an attempted bunt) which can be caught by an infielder with ordinary effort" when the bases are loaded or there are men on first and second with less than two out.

What if an outfielder is playing shallow and runs in to catch a pop-up in a situation where the infield-fly rule would normally apply? Since the ball was not caught by an infielder, should the rule be waived and can the outfielder therefore drop the ball and pull off a double play?

The rule book supplies the answer: "A ball is an infield fly, even if handled by an outfielder, if, in the umpire's judgment, the ball could as easily have been handled by an infielder."

So the book of baseball law is not elementary after all.

YOU BE THE UMPIRE!

Another definition in Rule 2.00: An inning "is that portion of a game . . . in which there are three putouts for each team."

But there can be four putouts during a club's turn at bat. Rule 7.10 describes a situation that "may require an umpire to recognize an apparent 'fourth out.' " It happened in a game between the Yankees and Brewers in July 1989 when a runner left a base too soon.

The argument over Don Denkinger's '85 World Series call was a doozy, but the issue was simple: Did the runner arrive at first base before the ball? The plays unfolding in this book go beyond the question of whether the ump was, or was not, blind on a particular play. They all involve the rule book—a document that is simple yet complicated, a code of conduct that belabors the obvious, but confounds the untutored.

An umpire of yesteryear named Bill Guthrie is supposed to have said, "It's nothing till I call it." Yet when the rules are concerned, it might be nothing even after the umpire has spoken.

Although any decision involving an ump's judgment "is final," a manager can file a protest with the league president if he thinks there is "reasonable doubt" over an umpire's interpretation of a rule. Once in a while, a protest is upheld.

But sometimes the rule book—and the civilized conduct of baseball it prescribes—are swept aside by

PREFACE

the passion of the moment and the prejudice of the day. Umpire Tim Hurst—the fellow who hurled those beer mugs back at the fans—was eventually fired after a rip-roaring argument with Columbia graduate and future Hall of Famer Eddie Collins. Their confrontation had concluded with Hurst spitting in the ballplayer's eye.

Hurst later explained his aggression: "I don't like college boys."

1

THE BALLPARK

The longest home run in baseball history came off the bat of the Babe.

But it wasn't Babe Ruth.

In April 1943, the New York Giants met their Jersey City farm club in an exhibition game at the Lakehurst Naval Air Station in New Jersey. The infield had three bases and a home plate, but the outfield wasn't so conventional. There were no fences. The ball field was a vast dirt expanse designed for the landing of aircraft, not baseballs.

When the Giants' Babe Barna walloped a ball over the head of Jersey City outfielder Howie Moss, the drive kept going. The baseball landed 450 feet from home plate, then rolled for another 200 feet before Moss caught up with it. Barna circled the bases and then a jeep was dispatched to retrieve Moss while he caught his breath.

YOU BE THE UMPIRE!

Barna, who would hit 9 homers in his major league career —only 705 fewer than the other Babe—had performed a mighty feat. But a look at the rule book would put a damper on his deed: Strictly speaking, he wasn't playing baseball at all.

The first sentence of the rule book says that "baseball is a game between two teams of nine players each, under direction of a manager, played on an enclosed field."

Lakehurst Naval Air Station aside, ballparks have been enclosed by fences since the 1860s. The quirkier ones like Fenway's Green Monster and Ebbets Field's crazy-angled, sign-splattered guardian of Bedford Avenue have brought great charm to the game. But when ball strikes wall, some delicious arguments have been hatched as well.

The rule book has plenty to say about the fences and the outfield dimensions. It does, however, leave room for imagination despite the worst efforts of "cookie-cutter" stadium architects.

But when the infield is concerned, there's nary an inch leeway to go astray.

Ty Cobb surely wouldn't let anyone have an inch's edge on him. While barnstorming in Cuba following the 1910 season, Cobb raised a storm when he was thrown out attempting to steal on a throw by Bruce Petway, a star catcher of the Negro leagues. Cobb protested that second base had been planted too far from first base. A tape measure was brought out, and it proved him right—it was ninety feet three inches down the line.

When it comes to the pitcher's mound, the rule book is no less precise than with the basepath layout. The Yankees' Cat-

THE BALLPARK

fish Hunter claimed the mound was too steep, causing him control problems, when he was beaten by the Brewers at Milwaukee's County Stadium one day in April 1976. Yankee Manager Billy Martin demanded a measurement, so the league's umpiring supervisor, John Stevens, did a personal survey.

The mound was contoured just as it was supposed to be: From a point six inches in front of the rubber to a point six feet toward home plate, it must uniformly descend one inch for every foot.

The rule book also deals with the condition of the playing field, but here the umpires have the final say.

When is it too muddy to continue?

One dark and drizzly afternoon at Braves Field in September 1949, Boston shortstop Connie Ryan tried to persuade Umpire George Barr to call things off in the fifth inning with his team trailing the Dodgers, 8–0. Moments later it would become an official game.

Ryan didn't say a thing to Barr, but he quickly found himself ordered to experience a full-fledged shower—and it wasn't with rainwater. Ryan had embellished his red-and-gray flannel wardrobe. He'd arrived in the on-deck circle sporting a long black raincoat.

Wrigley Field's ivy-covered center-field wall figured in a bizarre play during the 1945

YOU BE THE UMPIRE!

World Series. Strange doings were entirely appropriate that October, since the ballplayers themselves were an odd collection. With World War II bringing an exodus of big leaguers into military service, the pennant-winning Chicago Cubs and Detroit Tigers were mostly a collection of old-timers, 4-Fs, and mediocrities. (Detroit's Hank Greenberg and Virgil Trucks, both released from military service in '45, did, however, provide a touch of class.)

A wonderful example of the bumbling came in the bottom of the ninth inning of Game 5 when the Cubs' Phil Cavarretta hit a routine fly ball. Tiger right fielder Roy Cullenbine and center fielder Doc Cramer (the record book said he was forty years old but he claimed to be forty-three) let the baseball drop between them for a double.

Cramer's explanation: "I could have caught the ball, but Cullenbine kept shouting, 'All right, all right.' When I heard this I stopped, and then to my surprise, the ball plopped to the ground. I asked Cullenbine why he didn't make the catch, and he told me, 'When I called all right, all right, I meant all right, you catch it.' "

That was the second time in the ninth inning that Cullenbine had touched off wacky doings in the outfield. The first time, he was the batter. In the top of the ninth, with the Tigers leading by 6–3, Cramer was hit by a pitch from Paul Erickson. Greenberg followed with his third double of the game, a smash to left-center sending Cramer scurrying to third on his 40-plus legs.

Now Cullenbine stepped to the plate. It was a warm, sunny afternoon with the famous Wrigley Field wind blowing out to center field. Cullenbine hit the ball over the head of Andy Pafko, the center fielder, and the baseball landed on the fly amid the ivy. Then it disappeared. Pafko frantically tore into the vines, searching in vain for a bit of white amid the green, as the runners continued on their merry way.

How Far Could Cullenbine Get?

He was given a double as Cramer and Greenberg scored. Any fair ball that sticks in a fence or scoreboard—on the fly or after bouncing—is an automatic two bases.

What if a baseball—instead of sticking in a fence—goes right through it?

At Montreal's Delorimer Downs, the home of the old Royals of the International League, a porthole was drilled in the outfield wall. A batter hitting a ball through it was rewarded by the sponsor of the hole, Pal razor blades. He got a two-year supply. But a hitter zeroing in on the porthole would be doubly blessed. He also got a double, since any baseball going through an opening in a fence is—like a ball stuck in a fence—good for two bases.

In July 1964, a ball went through a hole in the Cleveland Stadium fence not as a result of the batter's prowess but an outfielder's clumsiness. The Washington Senators' Don Zimmer hit a ball that bounced off the right-field fence and then was accidentally kicked through a small opening by Indian right fielder Chico Salmon. The Senators' manager, Gil Hodges, argued that Zimmer deserved a home run, but the umpires disagreed. It was only a rule-book double.

The right-field wall at Ebbets Field is fondly remembered for the Abe Stark clothing store advertisement at the base of the scoreboard. HIT SIGN, WIN SUIT it dared the batters. But Stark wouldn't be parting with many suits at his Pitkin Avenue shop. The sign was placed at a spot that was virtually impossible to hit on the fly.

Back in 1923, it was a case of "hit flag, win argument" at Ebbets Field. When the Dodgers played host to the Boston Braves for a July Fourth doubleheader, the occasion was celebrated with fireworks. But in the sixth inning of the second game, it was the Braves' tempers that exploded. They could hardly believe what they had seen.

Jack Fournier, the Brooklyn first baseman, hit a drive to right-center field. The ball struck a flag flying atop the high wall, momentarily became entangled in the folds flapping in the breeze, dropped onto the top of the wall and then bounced back to the outfield grass.

Billy Southworth, the Braves' right fielder (he'd be their manager in the 1940s), grabbed the ball and fired it back to the infield. Fournier stopped at second base but Umpire Bob Hart waved him to the plate, ruling it was a home run.

The Braves argued, but the umpires were unmoved, so

THE BALLPARK

Boston Manager Fred Mitchell played the game under protest. After the Dodgers won, 9–5, the dispute went to John Heydler, the National League president.

Was Fournier Entitled to His Home Run?

The Braves insisted that the flagpole—and therefore the flag itself—were fixtures on the wall and therefore part of it so the ball should have remained in play.

Heydler drew an analogy in arriving at his decision. He said that if a vendor had left his basket atop a railing or a fence—or if any other artificial obstruction had been placed in such a spot—any ball hitting it and falling back would be a homer.

He ruled that the flag was a similar artificial obstruction since ground rules defining the barriers at ball parks customarily made no mention of flagstaffs atop fences. The flags, he noted, could be taken down on any particular day.

So flag-waving on Independence Day could not foil the Dodgers' Jack Fournier. His homer, and the Dodger victory, remained in the record books.

In mid-September of 1959, the Dodgers and Braves were arguing once more over a drive that cleared a barrier and then bounced back. But the geography had changed considerably. This time the scene of the dispute was the Los Angeles Coliseum.

Brooklyn and Boston—oops, Los Angeles and Milwaukee—were battling for a pennant along with the New York (make that San Francisco) Giants. With Johnny Podres pitching for the Dodgers, Joe Adcock slammed a shot that cleared the Coliseum's left-field screen and struck a supporting cable above and behind it. The ball bounded off the cable and then became stuck in the screen.

Did Adcock Have a Homer?

The Braves' first baseman toured the bases and entered his dugout to much backslapping and handshaking. But Umpire Frank Dascoli called him back, and it wasn't to take an extra bow. Adcock would have to settle for a double.

Fred Haney, the Braves' manager, argued that since the baseball had gone over the screen—no great feat since it was only 251 feet down the line—it didn't matter that the ball caromed back. But he got as much satisfaction as another Fred—Braves Manager Fred Mitchell—had received back in 1923 in the ball-in-the-flag dispute.

This time the ground rules won the day for the Dodgers. In the argument at Ebbets Field back in '23, the league president decided that the flag atop the right-field wall wasn't part of the fence since the ground rules made no mention of it.

But the Los Angeles Coliseum ground rules clearly

stated that any ball hitting the cable above the screen was in play. If the ball rebounded onto the screen and lodged there—as it had with Adcock's drive—it would be scored a double. If it bounced back onto the field, the batter was on his own.

"It's all here right in black and white," explained Dodger Manager Walter Alston afterward, pulling out the card listing the ground rules.

These rules—a different set for each ballpark—are apart from the regulations in the "Official Playing Rules." So long as they don't conflict with the general baseball rules, they're the law of that particular land where the game is being played.

"When we refer to the screen we call it The Thing," Alston would explain. "It's all considered one thing—towers, cables and screen."

The Braves, who went on to lose the game by 8–7, considered it robbery.

Two weeks later, the ball clubs were back at the Coliseum in Game 2 of a pennant playoff. The Dodgers would win again, wrapping up the National League title. That time, the Braves couldn't complain over a homer that wasn't. The Dodgers scored the winning run on a wild throw.

YOU BE THE UMPIRE!

The Oakland A's were taking batting practice one evening in April 1981 before their game with the Mariners at Seattle's Kingdome when Billy Martin noticed something strange in the white lines around home plate.

Billy was an expert on bending or breaking the rules. This time, however, it wasn't Martin but the opposing manager who was trying a slick maneuver. The batter's box seemed designed for the strides of giants—not the ones who played across San Francisco Bay from Martin's team but the anatomical variety.

Martin asked Bill Kunkel, the chief of the game's umpiring crew, to check the length of the box. Kunkel measured it at seven feet.

Did the Mariners Break Any Rules?

Although the rule book isn't too overbearing when it comes to the outfield, it is excruciatingly exact with other dimensions.

Two numbers have achieved almost mystical status: the layout of 90 feet between the bases and 60 feet 6 inches from the pitcher's rubber to home plate.

The other dimensions are little known except to grounds keepers, umpires and those managers who pass for baseball intellectuals.

THE BALLPARK

A few figures that every schoolboy cannot recite:
Home plate to second base: 127 feet, 3⅜ inches.
The pitcher's rubber: 24 inches by 6 inches.
The distance from dugouts to foul lines: at least 25 feet.
As for the batter's box, it must be 4 feet wide and 6 feet long.

Maury Wills, the Mariners' manager back in April '81, had decreed that an extra foot—in the direction of the pitcher's mound—be added to the box, and the head grounds keeper did the dirty work with the chalk marks.

The umpires didn't go so far as forfeiting the game to the Athletics when they discovered the tampering. They simply had the grounds keepers shrink the box back to its proper length.

Wills said he ordered the extra-large size because the Athletics had complained earlier in the series that the Mariners' Tom Paciorek was stepping out of the box toward the pitcher when he was hitting the ball.

Martin noted that his pitcher that night, Rick Langford, specialized in breaking balls. By moving up an extra foot in the box, Seattle batters could take their cuts before the baseballs broke.

Langford wasn't exactly unhittable that evening, but he was good enough, pitching a complete-game 7–4 victory.

Three days later, American League President Lee MacPhail suspended Wills for two games and fined him five hundred dollars for "doctoring the batter's box."

(In his playing days, Wills himself had been the target of creative grounds-keeping. Back in the 1960s, when he broke the major league base-stealing record as a Los Angeles Dodger, the Giants were accused of wetting down their infield to keep him from running wild.)

Wills would not have much longer beyond that Oakland series to think up extralegal ways to win as a manager. Eleven days after the batter's box episode, the Mariners fired him.

The Washington Senators found a creative way to stop Ted Williams—and it required nothing in the way of pitching talent.

One afternoon in August 1941, with the Senators leading the Red Sox, 6–3, in the eighth inning of a game at Washington's Griffith Stadium, Williams was at the plate with Joe Cronin on first base when it began to pour. The umps called time.

Now the grounds keepers did their part to help the home team—they sprang into inaction, making no effort to put the tarpaulin down.

It was only a shower, but thirty minutes later, when the rain had slackened, there was bad news for the Red Sox. Home-plate umpire George Pipgras stuck his toe into the baseline, came up muddied and called it a day.

Ruling that the field was unplayable, Pipgras awarded Washington an abbreviated victory.

The Red Sox protested that it wasn't their fault the field

was in no condition for any heroics by Williams or his teammates.

What Should the Final Score Be?

It wound up a shutout for the Red Sox. American League President Will Harridge awarded the game to Boston on a forfeit—an automatic 9–0 score—because the grounds keepers hadn't covered the field.

The rule book says that when play is halted, the game will be forfeited to the visitors if "the orders of the umpire to grounds keepers respecting preparation of the field for resumption of play are not complied with."

An old schoolboy's refrain tells how George Washington was "first in war, first in peace, first in the hearts of his countrymen." The futile Senator teams of the 1940s and '50s inspired a slightly different theme. The baseball–playing Washington was dubbed "first in war, first in peace, last in the American League." Not even a loyal grounds-keeping crew could remedy that state of affairs.

The home team—as the Washington Senators learned—has responsibility for the condition of its playing field. So what happens if a visiting ball club insists that conditions are unsafe?

YOU BE THE UMPIRE!

The Baltimore Orioles, battling for a pennant with the Yankees in September 1977, were playing the Blue Jays at Toronto. In the bottom of the fourth, the Jays broke a scoreless tie by coming up with four runs. Oriole Manager Earl Weaver, already in foul temper over the scoreboard, soon turned his wrath on the playing surface.

A steady rain was falling, so a tarpaulin had been placed over the pitcher's mound in the Toronto bull pen. In most parks, the bull pens are behind a fence, but at Exposition Park they were in foul territory. Weaver contended that his left fielder, Andres Mora, might stumble and be seriously injured if he tried to run down a foul fly and got his spikes caught on the tarp. Mora had slipped going into foul territory the night before, so he evidently was not too sure-footed to begin with.

When the Orioles took the field in the bottom of the fifth, Weaver demanded that Marty Springstead, the third-base umpire, order removal of the tarpaulin. Springstead was willing to have the tarp folded back halfway but Weaver was in no mood for compromise. Before the inning's first pitch could be thrown, he pulled his players off the field. Springstead suggested that Weaver play the game under protest, but that didn't mollify him either. So the umpire gave the Orioles fifteen minutes to return. When time was up, they were still sulking in their dugout.

THE BALLPARK

What Should the Ump Have Done?

Springstead gave the Blue Jays a forfeit victory. "We didn't have a team to play, so that was it," he explained. Although Toronto had an obligation to maintain safe conditions, it was up to the umpires to determine what was and was not a hazard. Once Springstead ordered the Orioles to resume the game, their argument was over. A team forfeits when it "is unable or refuses to place nine players on the field."

Weaver's funk would prove costly to the Orioles' pennant chances. His ball club finished two and a half games behind the Yankees.

The following July, Weaver was thrown out of a game by Springstead for the sixth time. (It was his sixtieth ejection in ten years.)

Weaver's opinion of Springstead after that encounter: "He's a guy with no brains who makes up the rules as he goes along."

Springstead's response: "He's no Marilyn Monroe. Do you think I want to look at that midget every day?"

If it's not the wind, it's the rain. So went the Mets' complaint after they dropped a Sunday doubleheader at Candlestick Park in May 1977. The debacle concluded with Mets pitcher Jon Matlack mad at the ball club's management while management was mad at the umpires.

The Mets dropped the opener, 4–2, for their sixth loss in seven games and then Matlack took the mound for the second game.

Manager Joe Frazier had juggled his lineup by putting Lenny Randle at second base in place of Felix Millan, Leo Foster at third base for Randle, and Mike Vail in left field replacing Ed Kranepool.

Normally bedeviled by winds that can turn an outfield fly into an infield pop-up, Candlestick was the scene of havoc this time because of a steady rain.

Frazier's lineup creativity would combine with the elements to undo Matlack early on.

After two singles and an intentional walk had loaded the bases for the Giants in the first inning with one down, Willie McCovey hit a potential double-play grounder to Randle. The new second baseman promptly threw the ball into the outfield, and Vail, the new left fielder, kicked it around. Instead of Matlack being out of the inning, all the runners scored and he was down 3–0. In the second inning, center fielder Lee Mazzilli slipped on the wet carpet chasing down a liner hit by Giant pitcher John Curtis, who made it all the way home on a triple and an error.

As the game moved along, the Mets seemed to be in quicksand. They kept sinking as the rains made the field swampy and the Giants kept pouring it on.

The umps ordered sand put down on the mound, but it was little help for Matlack. The left-hander was kept out there until the sixth inning—risking injury in a game that was out of reach—and by time the Mets batted in the seventh they were being humiliated by 10–0.

In the top of the seventh, the Mets' pratfalls continued as Mazzilli slipped and fell, turning himself into a human mudball, swinging at a pitch. At that point, home-plate Umpire Dutch Rennert had seen enough. He decided the field had become unsafe and was convinced the ground crew could do nothing to make it playable again that afternoon. So he instantly called the game.

Joe McDonald, the Mets' general manager, protested the defeat. He argued that the umps should have ended things in the early going, since the field was a muddy mess virtually from the second game's outset. That, of course, would have wiped out the Giants' big lead because the Mets had to bat five times to make it an official game.

Was the Game Properly Called Off?

The National League president, Chub Feeney, did overrule his umps, but not the way the Mets wanted it.

Should the second game have even gotten under way? That was a decision for the umpires to make. The home team's right to call off a game because of poor weather conditions does not apply to the second game of doubleheaders.

Once the second game had begun, it was up to the home-plate umpire to decide whether the field remained playable. A league president would not be eager to overrule the umpire's judgment, and Feeney didn't do so.

But he did rule that the umps neglected to wait a specified amount of time before calling the game. The rule book requires a thirty-minute wait, even in awful weather conditions, but the umps at Candlestick had ended things right after Mazzilli went down in the mud.

So Feeney put the Giants' victory on hold and ordered that the game be resumed—with Mazzilli still at the plate —the next time the Mets visited San Francisco.

Now the Mets surrendered. Rebuffed in their bid to have the entire game replayed, they decided not to drag things out. They withdrew their protest and accepted a 10–0 drubbing.

But Matlack was not so charitable. When the Mets— now in last place—returned to New York after that doubleheader, he asked to be traded. Already convinced that management was running the franchise down, he was steaming over the soggy afternoon at Candlestick.

"We were slipping all over the place," Matlack noted, but "the manager never complained until after the game."

Matlack would suffer arm troubles that year and finish at 7–15. The ball club didn't do any better, winding up in the cellar.

The next year, the Mets would free Matlack, sending him to the Texas Rangers. But he did outlast the manager who'd left him out to dry in the Candlestick rain. Joe Frazier had been fired forty-four games into the '77 season.

THE BALLPARK

"They were just uncontrollable beasts," lamented a shaken Nestor Chylak after surviving the most violent mood swing an umpire had ever encountered.

In the early innings, while umpiring at home plate in a June 1974 night game between the Indians and Texas Rangers at Cleveland Stadium, Chylak had been the amorous objective of a fan. A woman came out of the stands and attempted to kiss him. Rare though it was for an ump to be loved, Chylak avoided her advances.

By the ninth inning, the crowd's emotions had veered to the other extreme: Chylak was hit on the head as hundreds of fans swarmed onto the field and fighting broke out between spectators and players.

The mayhem had nothing to do with Chylak's calling of balls and strikes. It had everything to do with that evening's promotional event: Beer Night.

The Indians had sold 65,000 containers of beer (ten-ounce size) at ten cents apiece. By time the crowd of 23,134 had dried up the supply, the ballpark had become a miniature war zone.

The early ingredients for a riot had actually been brewed at Arlington Stadium in Texas. Exactly one week before, the Indian and Ranger players had fought there after a fan doused a Cleveland player with suds. So Indian fans were in a hostile mood by time the first pitch was thrown on their own turf. The drinking that was to come would unloose whatever inhibitions remained.

YOU BE THE UMPIRE!

After the second inning, forty fans ran across the field, some of them doing somersaults. A streaker clad only in one sock vaulted the left-field fence and was last seen being pursued by a policeman. In the seventh inning the Ranger pitchers were evacuated from their bull pen to the dugout after being the target of firecrackers. Billy Martin, the Texas manager, broke a bat trying to chase away fans on his dugout roof. In the midst of all this, smoke bombs were set off in the stands.

In the ninth, a half-dozen fans leapt out of the right-field stands and accosted Ranger outfielder Jeff Burroughs after a sacrifice fly by the Indians' John Lowenstein tied the game at 5–5. Players from both clubs—now uniting in the face of a common enemy—ran out to protect Burroughs. Within seconds, hundreds of fans spilled onto the field and it became a battleground. Cleveland pitcher Tom Hilgendorf was hit on the head with a steel chair, Ranger players Mike Hargrove and Duke Sims fought with a fan on the pitcher's mound, and Umpire Chylak was attacked.

The Indians had two men on base with two out in a tie game, but they would send no more runners across the plate that evening. The beleaguered Chylak stopped the game. The only action for the rest of the night would involve the police and any fans they could catch.

THE BALLPARK

How Should the Game Have Gone into the Record Books?

The Indian players couldn't be blamed for the fans' frenzy, but the ball club's management could indeed be held responsible. So Chylak declared a forfeit, giving the Rangers a 9–0 victory.

The rule book says "the home team shall provide police protection sufficient to preserve order." If spectators interfere with play and the field is not cleared within a reasonable amount of time, the umpire is permitted to forfeit the game to the visiting team.

Were the Indians' front-office executives embarrassed? Not nearly enough to stop them from protesting the forfeit. The club's general manager, Phil Seghi, asked the American League to overrule Chylak because the umpires had not warned the fans that their mayhem could bring a forfeit. Seghi also contended that the umpires should have made a greater effort to have the police clear the field.

The protest was dismissed and so the game would be another defeat for the perennially downtrodden Indians, who presumably had driven their fans to drink long before the riotous events of Beer Night.

YOU BE THE UMPIRE!

The Yankees won four straight World Series titles from 1936 to '39, dominating baseball with the likes of Gehrig, DiMaggio, Dickey, Gomez and Ruffing.

But on the afternoon of Sunday, September 3, 1939, they played perhaps the worst few moments of baseball ever seen.

The Yanks and Red Sox went to the eighth inning of a doubleheader nightcap at Fenway Park tied, 5–5. New York quickly struck for two runs and had George Selkirk on third base and Joe Gordon on second with one out. Then strange things began to happen.

There was a 6:30 P.M. Sunday curfew in Boston. Play could not continue beyond that time, and if the moment arrived in the midst of an inning, the score at the end of the previously completed inning would be the result.

By time the Yanks had taken their 7–5 lead, less than ten minutes remained before the curfew would be invoked. So New York was suddenly frantic to complete its turn at bat and then retire the Red Sox. If the inning couldn't be completed, the game would revert to a 5–5 tie.

The Red Sox were determined to delay. The Boston manager, Joe Cronin, ordered pitcher Joe Heving to intentionally walk the next Yankee batter, Babe Dahlgren. The Yankee manager, Joe McCarthy, told Dahlgren to swing at anything and ordered his runners to erase themselves. On the first pitch, Dahlgren whiffed at a ball way out of the strike zone as Selkirk trotted in from third base. Johnny Peacock, the Red Sox catcher, instinctively tagged Selkirk though he would have been better off letting him score. On the second wide pitch, Gordon ambled to home plate, where Peacock tagged him for the third out.

Cronin quickly accosted Umpire Cal Hubbard, complaining that the Yanks were making a mockery of the game. That incited the crowd of 27,000, and soon pop bottles and straw hats were sent flying onto the field. It was impossible to clear the debris in the few minutes left before the curfew took effect.

For Whom Did the Curfew Toll a Defeat?

Hubbard, holding the Red Sox responsible for the fans' wrath, declared a 9–0 forfeit victory for the Yankees. He invoked the rule on crowd control that Umpire Chylak would cite thirty-five years later in that Indians-Rangers fiasco.

But the Red Sox protested to American League President Will Harridge, claiming that the Yankees had acted unfairly by deliberately running into putouts and trying to nullify a perfectly legal intentional walk.

Boston's argument was persuasive. Harridge called the actions of Dahlgren, Selkirk and Gordon "reprehensible," fined them a hundred dollars apiece, vacated the forfeit and ordered the game replayed.

YOU BE THE UMPIRE!

It's illegal to use "tactics palpably designed to delay or shorten the game."

The Yankees had speeded things up—in effect, trying to shorten the game—by turning their base runners into human sacrifices. So the league president ruled that the spectators' conduct, although interfering with play, was outweighed by the Yanks' conduct, which had made a travesty of the game.

The Yankees had come out second best this time. But when the season was over, they could laugh last. They finished a mere seventeen games ahead of the second-place Red Sox.

2

ON THE MOUND

It began with a furtive snapping of the wrists and with a flight of clamshells: Pitchers were figuring out ways to get an edge on the batters while baseball was still in its dawn.

In the game's first decades, the pitchers were more like lobbers. They were required to toss the ball underhand with a stiff wrist, and so the baseball came in slow and straight, a batter's delight.

But by 1860, a teenager named James Creighton was defying the rule book. Pitching for Brooklyn's powerful Excelsiors, he used a barely noticeable arm-bend and wrist-snap that allowed him to put speed and spin on the ball.

Three years later, fourteen-year-old Arthur Cummings made a wonderful discovery. "A number of boys and myself were amusing ourselves by throwing clamshells and watching them sail along through the air, turning now to the right and now to the left," he would recall years later.

If a clamshell can wiggle, why not a baseball? young Arthur thought. Although he weighed only 120 pounds, "Candy" Cummings would go on to win 124 games in pro baseball during the 1870s with his marvelous invention: the curveball.

As baseball sought a balance between pitcher and batter, the rules kept changing. Virtually all restrictions on the pitching motion were dropped in 1884, and three years after that, batters lost the privilege of instructing the pitcher where to put the ball: high, low or in between.

But even after the rules gave them a fair chance to foil the batters, the baseball descendants of Creighton and Cummings kept scheming.

Soon after the turn of the century, a minor league ballplayer named George Hildebrand discovered that a moist baseball could do amazing things on its route to the plate. He taught the trick to a seemingly over-the-hill pitcher named Elmer Stricklett, who was sinking into oblivion in the Pacific Coast League. In 1904, finding magic in his salivary glands, Stricklett made it to the Chicago White Sox. He soon shared the secret, becoming the father of big league spitballers.

By the end of World War I, the pitchers had gone far beyond drooling. The more sophisticated types used paraffin or talcum to smooth the baseball so it would slip off the fingers easily while a twist was applied (the "shine ball"). For those favoring a contrary theory, a piece of sandpaper roughened the baseball so it dipped and darted in flight (the "emery ball").

ON THE MOUND

In 1920, the rules-makers struck back, banning all freakish deliveries. The seventeen pitchers who were throwing the spitter at the time were, however, allowed to keep using it until they retired.

The final survivor was Burleigh Grimes, a future Hall of Famer. In 1934, he'd deliver baseball's last spitball.

More precisely, it was the last "legal" spitball. In the decades since Burleigh drew his last moist baseball breath, many a pitcher has been accused of scuffing the ball or loading it up. But convictions have been rare: Only five pitchers have been suspended for cheating.

The rule book looks beyond the baseball itself in keeping the pitchers from dominating the hitters. The anemic batting averages of the 1968 season brought a reduction in the height of the pitching rubber from fifteen inches to ten inches, where it has remained ever since. And the strike zone officially shrank as well, though one umpire's "strike" may be another's "ball."

The pitchers also have a miniwar going with base runners. Here, too, the rules-makers try to keep things fair. The balk regulations are designed to prevent pitchers from deceiving runners.

Sometimes the balk rules seem a little too tough. In Game 6 of the 1952 World Series, the Brooklyn Dodgers' Billy Loes was sailing along in the seventh inning with a 1–0 edge over the Yankees. Then he gave up a homer to Yogi Berra and a single to Gene Woodling. Presumably unnerved by now, Loes let the ball squirt out of his hands as he went into his motion against the next batter, Irv Noren. The baseball plopped to the ground a few feet behind him. "Balk," proclaimed the umps.

YOU BE THE UMPIRE!

Woodling was waved to second base, and later in the inning, Yankee pitcher Vic Raschi hit a one-hopper that caromed off Loes's leg and bounced toward right field, sending Woodling home with the tie-breaking run.

The Yanks went on to win the game, and the next day they won the Series. So the Dodgers had to "wait till next year" thanks in part to one of baseball's stranger balk calls.

Loes offered no excuse for letting the baseball slip from his fingers, but he definitely had an explanation for failing to nab Raschi's comebacker: He'd lost the ground ball in the sun.

The rule book lays out precise ingredients for a baseball. It says "the ball shall be a sphere formed by yarn wound around a small core of cork, rubber or similar material, covered with two strips of white horsehide or cowhide, tightly stitched together." It sets the weight of balls at between 5 and 5¼ ounces and the circumference at between 9 and 9¼ inches.

Does that mean there's no way balls can be tampered with to give the pitcher an edge even before the teams take the field? A silly question.

In August 1965, the Chicago White Sox were accused of freezing baseballs before handing them over to the umpires.

Cold balls absorb more moisture than balls kept under normal temperature conditions and become heavier, thereby losing their "pop." Since the White Sox had few power hitters in '65 (their home-run leaders would be Bill Skowron and Johnny Romano, each with a grand total of 18), taking the rabbit out of the hide would be a wonderful equalizer.

In a late-summer four-game series between the White Sox and Tigers at Briggs Stadium, Detroit batters hit 13 home runs. But in a five-game series between the teams at Comiskey Park soon afterward, Detroit could not manage a single homer.

"I thought something was funny when the first two batters hit the ball and it went 'splat,' " complained Tiger pitcher Hank Aguirre after losing a 1–0 game in Chicago.

"I've never seen game balls like that," remarked Umpire Ed Hurley, who had been around for nineteen big-league seasons.

Should the White Sox's Dead-Ball Victory Have Remained Alive?

The umpires get their baseballs from the home team in sealed packages. They open the seals, then remove the gloss on the balls with specially prepared mud.

But there's no way the umps can prove a baseball has been frozen before the first pitch. That being the case, there's certainly no way to make a case against cowardly ball clubs afterward.

The accusation against Chicago was considered by American League President Joe Cronin. But he could hardly figure out the edge the White Sox would get, let alone do something about it.

"It seems to me that no matter what the condition of the ball, it would be as fair for one team as the other," said Cronin.

After missing the point, Cronin decided on a fishing expedition guaranteed to miss finding any frozen baseballs. He ordered that the storerooms of the league's ten ball clubs be inspected.

If any baseballs were sitting in freezers when Cronin warned of inspections, they no doubt were provided with enough zip by clubhouse men to hop right out.

The furor over the frozen balls would quickly die away, but the White Sox' dead-ball victory would live on in the record books.

Chris Pelekoudas was in his twentieth year of umpiring by the summer of 1968. Having seen thousands of pitches approach him, he surely knew when a baseball was doing tricks surpassing the natural talents of the man on the mound.

On the afternoon of August 18, Pelekoudas observed some wonderful dips and doodles from his vantage point behind home plate when the Cubs took on the Cincinnati Reds in the first game of a Wrigley Field doubleheader.

He could find no physical evidence of cheating, so he

ON THE MOUND

relied on what his eyes told him. Four times he would accuse Cub reliever Phil Regan of loading up the baseball.

The arguing erupted in the seventh inning, right after Regan came in with the Reds leading, 2–1. After Regan's first delivery to pinch-hitter Mack Jones acted strangely, Pelekoudas warned him that he was throwing an illegal pitch and ordered him to stop. On the very next pitch, Pelekoudas called an automatic "ball," accusing Regan of again loading up the baseball. Then, after Jones flied to center field on a 2-and-2 pitch, Pelekoudas nullified the out and once more called a "ball" on grounds Regan had delivered a wet one.

Now Umpire Shag Crawford, the crew chief, got a towel and wiped the inside of Regan's cap and his forehead. He claimed to find Vaseline, although none of the baseballs Regan had thrown were found to have anything other than cowhide on them.

Jones eventually grounded out, but in the furor the umps had created, Cub Manager Leo Durocher was tossed from the game.

In the ninth inning, Pelekoudas struck again, ruling that a pitch Pete Rose missed for strike three was another tainted delivery. He called it a "ball" and then Rose, allowed to try again, delivered a single amid a shower of debris from Cub fans.

Randy Hundley, the Chicago catcher, was thrown out of the game arguing that ruling. (Moments later, Rose showed his gratitude to the umps by hurling his helmet when he was called out by Umpire John Kibler while trying to steal second. He, too, was ejected.)

39

But Regan was not tossed out.

Pelekoudas said afterward that he had planned to eject the pitcher but "then I had second thoughts. I said, 'To hell with him. Let him stay in the game and suffer.' Every illegal pitch will be a ball."

The ump decided what was an illegal pitch by watching the flight of the ball. He maintained that Regan's pitches were breaking down without any spin, a sure sign that he was throwing a spitball or a greaser and not a sinker.

"I've been umpiring long enough to know an illegal pitch when I see one," Pelekoudas said afterward. "We're not stupid. We can spot an illegal pitch. Anyone can spot one. Even the spectators can tell."

Was Regan Rightfully Convicted?

Pelekoudas and his fellow umps were ahead of their times.

Back in 1968, an umpire had to catch a pitcher in the act in order to charge him with wetting the ball in violation of Rule 8.02, the major "no-no" clause regarding illegal deliveries. An umpire would not accuse a pitcher of an illegal delivery unless he saw him putting his hands to his mouth.

But Pelekoudas and the other umps in his crew decided they would take action as soon as a suspicious delivery was spotted regardless of whether they found any evidence.

"They've been screaming about enforcing the rules," Pelekoudas said. "Well, we're going to enforce them."

But tradition does not die easily in baseball. The Cubs

ON THE MOUND

protested the game—a 2–1 defeat—to National League President Warren Giles.

Two days later, Giles arrived at Wrigley Field to conduct an investigation. He didn't uphold the protest, but after meeting with Durocher and Regan, Giles came away singing the pitcher's praises.

Calling Regan "a gentleman," Giles said that "Phil has told me he did not have Vaseline or any other lubricant on his sweatband and I believe him."

What Giles didn't reveal was that he had spoken earlier in the day with Pelekoudas by phone and had told him, along with his umpiring crew chief, Shag Crawford, that they should no longer call an illegal pitch unless they had evidence that a foreign substance had been applied to the ball.

Regan was exonerated and he would go on to lead the National League in saves with 21 and win the Fireman Award as the top relief pitcher.

It would take six more years, but the umpires finally got the weapon that Pelekoudas had prematurely claimed.

Rule 8.02 (a) says that a pitcher shall not "apply a foreign substance of any kind to the ball" or "expectorate on the ball, either hand, or his glove" or "deliver what it is called the . . . 'spit' ball."

In 1974 the umps were permitted at last to pronounce guilt under this rule without getting physical evidence.

Now, suspicion is enough. If an ump believes that a pitcher is loading up the baseball, he first must call the delivery a "ball" and issue a warning. A second suspected spitter brings an automatic ejection.

YOU BE THE UMPIRE!

But even with the discretion given to the umpires, there has been only one ejection for spitballing since the Regan-Pelekoudas dispute.

In his 1974 autobiography *Me and the Spitter,* Gaylord Perry confessed to having loaded up the ball, though he claimed in the book that he'd reformed. Eight years later, by then forty-three years old and pitching for the Seattle Mariners, Perry was tossed from a game with the Red Sox and given a ten-day suspension for going back to his old tricks, which many baseball people believed he'd never abandoned.

Perry joined an exclusive club. Since the spitball and other exotic deliveries were outlawed in 1920, just two pitchers have been suspended for throwing a spitball. Before Perry's banishment, only Nelson Potter of the '44 St. Louis Browns had served a ten-day ban. But Potter's season ended happily. He was part of the pitching staff that brought the Browns the only pennant in their half-century of futility.

When Don Sutton took the mound for the Dodgers against the Cardinals at Busch Stadium the night of July 14, 1978, he was seeking his two hundredth career victory. This would indeed be a memorable evening, but not the way he envisioned it.

Trailing by 2–1, Sutton got the final out of the seventh

inning when Mike Tyson flied to Rick Monday in right field. But then Doug Harvey, the chief of the umpiring crew, called for the baseball. Moments later, he told the Cardinals, who were returning to the field, to get back to their dugout. Harvey called the final pitch to Tyson a ball, then directed Tyson to return to the plate.

Harvey said later that he'd collected three Sutton-delivered baseballs with "a roughness on the ball almost in exactly the same spot" and "it was enough of a scuff to alter the flight of thc ball."

Harvey never accused Sutton of defacing the baseball himself. He merely contended that the pitcher had delivered balls that someone had defaced. The tampering supposedly continued even after Sutton had been warned, so it was time to act.

What's the Punishment for the Pitcher?

There are two rules designed to combat defacing of the baseball. (The aim is to eliminate unhittable zigs and zags. When a baseball is defaced, the airflow around it creates a befuddling traffic pattern as it approaches the plate.)

Rule 8.02 (a) says, among other things, that "the pitcher shall not . . . deface the ball in any manner." When there's a second offense after a warning, the pitcher is automatically ejected.

Rule 3.02 applies not simply to the pitcher, but to anybody on the field. It says that "no player shall intentionally discolor or damage the ball by rubbing it with soil, rosin, paraffin, licorice, sandpaper, emery paper or other foreign substance."

The umpire is supposed to eject the guilty party and remove the baseball from the game. But the penalty under 3.02 can be a lot tougher. What if the ump can't find the designated scuffer? If the pitcher then delivers a damaged or discolored ball, he gets a double penalty: ejection from the game and a ten-day suspension.

Since Harvey said several times that he wasn't accusing Sutton of defacing the ball, it seemed that the pitcher's punishment would fall under Rule 3.02, requiring a suspension for merely delivering a defaced baseball.

Harvey did eject Sutton, and then Tyson, the Cardinal batter he had just retired, came to the plate again. This time, against a hastily summoned Lance Rautzhan, Tyson once more flied to right. Now, the out counted.

What about the suspension?

Sutton would never miss a start. Dodger Manager Tommy Lasorda—contending there was nothing wrong with any of the balls Sutton threw—played the game under protest. But Sutton took more drastic action. After the game—a 4–1 Dodger loss—he announced plans to sue both Harvey and the National League for depriving him of his livelihood.

Three days later, National League President Chub Feeney announced that Sutton would not, in fact, be suspended. While restating that Sutton was "ejected for throwing a defaced baseball"—an act requiring a suspension under Rule 3.02—Feeney cited the other rule, 8.02 (a), as governing the case.

Was Feeney so shook up by the threat of a lawsuit that he couldn't get his rules straight? It's hard to say, since he refused to discuss how he'd arrived at his curious decision.

The next night, Sutton finally got victory No. 200, defeating the Pirates, 7–2, on a six-hitter. Underneath his jersey, he wore a sweatshirt with a scrawled phrase that proclaimed victory in more than one sense. The shirt read: NOT GUILTY.

Phil Regan in the 1960s and Don Sutton in the '70s got away lightly, but there would be a modest crackdown in the 1980s.

In addition to the suspension of Gaylord Perry for throwing a spitter, three pitchers would be ejected and then banned for ten days for carrying extracurricular equipment presumably designed to scuff the baseball.

The rogues' gallery:

—Rick Honeycutt of the Seattle Mariners, caught with a thumbtack sticking through a piece of tape on his glove's right index finger in a 1981 game against the Kansas City Royals. (He pleaded no contest.)

—Joe Niekro of the Minnesota Twins, who, when ordered by the umps to empty his pockets during a 1987 game against the California Angels, expelled an emery board and a piece of sandpaper. (He claimed he needed them to file his nails for his knuckleball.)

—Kevin Gross of the Philadelphia Phillies, found with sandpaper glued to the pocket of his glove while pitching in a 1987 game against the Chicago Cubs. (He insisted he wasn't scuffing the ball but merely "fooling" with the paper.)

In a game of baseball word-association, *pine tar* is invariably linked to George Brett. But don't tell that to Jay Howell.

When the Dodgers played the Mets at Shea Stadium in Game Three of the 1988 National League Championship Series, the conditions that Saturday afternoon were more suited for football than baseball. The night before, a heavy rain had fallen. Saturday came up damp and cold, the kind of day pitchers dread. But there were products to be pitched on national television and a play-off schedule to be kept, so the show would go on.

After seven and a half innings of shivering, the Dodgers held a 4–3 lead. Exit Orel Hershiser, the Los Angeles starter, and enter Jay Howell, the Dodgers' relief ace.

Howell led his club in saves with 21 and seemed to have come by them honestly—he had never been suspected of doing anything strange to the baseball in his seven-year big league career. But the right-hander would throw just five pitches this day before creating an uproar.

Howell had a count of 3 balls and 2 strikes on Kevin McReynolds when Mets Manager Davey Johnson asked home-plate Ump Joe West to take a closer look at the reliever. At issue: Howell's glove.

ON THE MOUND

Bill Robinson, the Mets' first-base coach, had become suspicious when Howell tugged at his glove, and he alerted Johnson. When the manager saw Howell repeat the tugging, he sprang off his bench to demand a surprise inspection.

West and the umpiring crew chief, Harry Wendelstedt, took Howell's glove and rubbed it. They determined there was substance to the Mets' complaint. A foreign substance, which turned out to be pine tar, had been smeared on the glove's heel.

What Should Come Next for Howell?

Howell said afterward that he wasn't seeking to make the baseball do tricks, nor was he trying to deface it. He simply wanted to get a good grip for his curveball amid abominable weather conditions. The rosin bag couldn't do the job because of a steady rain, so he'd applied the sticky pine tar to his glove and had rubbed the tar not-so-discreetly on his fingers.

The pine tar didn't even come off in a paste on his hand —rubbing the glove would only bring up some fine grains —but using it had violated the rule book.

Section 8.02 (b) declares: "The pitcher shall not have on his person, or in his possession, any foreign substance." The penalty for getting caught is "immediate ejection."

Unlike Rule 3.02, which forbids the delivery of a scuffed ball, 8.02 (b) does not carry an automatic suspension for violators. But it doesn't rule out a ban, either, as then

YOU BE THE UMPIRE!

National League President Bart Giamatti would soon make clear.

Howell was invited by the umps to spend the rest of the afternoon in the warmth of the Dodger clubhouse. The 3-and-2 count to McReynolds stood—none of the strikes could be called balls retroactively—but the Mets outfielder would finish off his at bat against another pitcher.

Howell's departure spelled disaster for the Dodgers. The Mets came up with five runs in the inning against Orlando Pena, Jesse Orosco and Ricky Horton and went on to an 8–4 victory, giving them a two-games-to-one lead in the series.

When Howell was ejected, Giamatti, seated near the Mets' dugout, asked the umpires to bring the tainted glove over for his inspection.

In his two years in office Giamatti had established a reputation as a law-and-order executive who would come down hard on anyone sullying the game he loved to wax lyrical over. He had suspended Pete Rose for thirty days for shoving an umpire and had ordered vigilant enforcement of the balk rules. When the Dodgers-Mets game was over, he had to decide whether to mete out further punishment to Howell.

The verdict: a three-game ban. Howell would not be allowed to pitch in Games 4 or 5 or in Game 6 if the series went that far.

"Mr. Howell would be eligible to pitch should there be a seventh game," announced Giamatti. "I do not want to see a championship ultimately decided for fans and teammates

—if the LCS goes seven games—by the accident of one man's mistakes."

(The series would, in fact, go to Game 7 and the Dodgers would win it, without needing help from Howell.)

The honor of being called "Mr." hardly outweighed the punishment so far as Howell was concerned.

He acknowledged knowing the pine tar was illegal, but claimed that pitchers commonly used it in harsh weather.

"It doesn't change the flight of the ball, it doesn't scuff the ball," he argued. "I thought at worst they would take the glove and throw it out of the game, give me another glove and let me go at it."

Dodger Manager Tommy Lasorda unsurprisingly saw things his pitcher's way. But he kept matters in perspective. Life was still to be savored, even without one's ace relief pitcher. The next afternoon (these were the days before he became a diet pitchman), Lasorda communed in his office with a container of lasagna that seemed to be saturated in cheese, tomato sauce, veal and sausages.

"Some of the other guys let their players drive 'em to drink," he mused. "Not me. My players drive me to pasta."

They called him "the Mad Monk." Russ Meyer, notorious for his temper, was never stormier than on the afternoon of May 25, 1952, pitching for the Brooklyn Dodgers against the Phillies at Shibe Park.

Meyer had been fuming over the ball-and-strike calls of Umpire Augie Donatelli. Finally, with outfielder Mel Clark at bat in the fourth inning, the right-hander rushed toward home plate for a direct confrontation.

Roy Campanella pushed him away from the ump, and Meyer retreated to the mound. Then he found another outlet for his aggression—the rosin bag. He heaved it thirty feet into the air. But that provided little comfort. The bag came down on Meyer's head.

When the Dust Cleared, Could Meyer Be Charged with an Infraction?

The pitcher can use the rosin bag only to dry his hands. He is not allowed to dust the baseball with rosin or apply it to his glove or any part of the uniform. The Russ Meyer buffoonery was hardly envisioned by the rules-makers, but by bringing the bag down upon his cap, he presumably violated the letter of the rosin-bag law.

The display of temper was, of course, what brought Meyer's ejection. As he trudged off, he flung his glove into the dugout. But that parting salute was hardly the last of Meyer so far as the TV cameras went.

Moments later, Philadelphia's WPTZ-TV showed Meyer making an obscene gesture at Donatelli from the dugout, not exactly the kind of television fare viewers of the early 1950s were accustomed to. The Philadelphia police commissioner, Thomas J. Gibbons, would receive dozens of angry letters and phone calls protesting Meyer's behavior. Responding to his constituents, the commissioner warned Meyer against any repetition of "indecent and disorderly conduct."

Had Meyer kept his temper in check, he would have been well rewarded that afternoon. In the eighth inning, the Dodgers assaulted Phillie starter Curt Simmons and four relievers for 12 runs before making an out, a record for most runs at the start of an inning. By then, instead of enjoying outrageous batting support, Meyer and his rosin-stained cap had long departed.

 Russ Meyer was a sweetie in comparison to Johnny Allen.

Allen made the Top 10 ranking when Bill Summers, a longtime American League umpire, compiled a list of "Baseball Boors I Have Known."

"Johnny Allen had an explosive fastball that he couldn't always control, and the same could be said of his disposition," Summers would recall. "John was mean enough to brush back Florence Nightingale."

On the afternoon of June 7, 1938, Allen was holding a 2–0 lead for the Cleveland Indians against the Red Sox at Fenway Park in the bottom of the first inning.

The right-hander retired the first two batters, but then

he walked Ben Chapman and gave up a homer to Jimmie Foxx. He ended the inning by striking out Joe Cronin, Boston's manager and shortstop.

Allen's mood had presumably turned foul when he'd lost his lead. But now Cronin would complain that the pitcher wasn't being quite fair, and Allen would lose his head as well.

Cronin groused to Bill McGowan, the home-plate umpire, about Allen's attire, specifically the right sleeve of his undershirt. It had been slit so the tatters waved in the breeze when he delivered the ball.

Was Allen Violating Anything Other than Neat Grooming Standards?

The rule book is, among other things, a fashion statement. It says that "no player shall wear ragged, frayed or slit sleeves."

A tattered sleeve is one more potential weapon for a pitcher. By slitting his sleeve—causing it to flap as he winds up—he can make it doubly tough on a batter trying to pick up the flight of the ball.

So McGowan ordered Allen to change his sweatshirt between innings.

Allen had previously been at odds with McGowan, who had a formidable reputation of his own for crustiness. Earlier in the season, the pitcher had been fined $25 for disputing the ump's ball-and-strike calls. Now, having seen his 2–0 lead disappear, Allen was about to be stripped of his clothing as well.

He went to the clubhouse—presumably to find a new undershirt—but after five minutes Indian Manager Oscar Vitt noticed that his pitcher had not reemerged.

When Vitt went to investigate, Allen told him he had no intention of going back out there. So the manager promptly slapped a $250 fine on his recluse and found himself a reliever.

American League President Will Harridge later fined Allen an additional $200. But Allen quickly got the money back in one of baseball's strangest promotional schemes. A Cleveland department store paid him for the privilege of displaying the notorious sweatshirt in its window.

Allen later moved on to the Brooklyn Dodgers. One day during the 1943 season, he would finally succeed in bringing about a baseball fashion change—but in the umpires' dress.

Leo Durocher, Allen's manager at Brooklyn, would recall how the pitcher jumped Umpire George Barr after a balk call against him in Pittsburgh. Allen pounded his baseball on the ump's bald head and then went on to sterner stuff.

"Barr is flat on his back and now Johnny has him by his necktie," Durocher remembered. "Barr was one of the umpires who wore those four-in-hand neckties. His tongue was hanging out and he was turning purple.

"I give you my word of honor that no umpire has worn a four-in-hand tie since."

Allen's big league pitching career ended in 1944. A few

years later, he would be wearing a different kind of uniform.

Durocher was in Columbus at the annual major league meetings when he spotted Allen at a hotel bar.

"Hey, John, what are you doing with yourself these days?" Durocher asked.

Allen replied: "I've gone to umpiring."

It's a summer scene guaranteed to spice the baseball highlights telecast every few days: A pitcher throws the ball inside and then the batter charges the mound, enraged that the ball came within a foot of him.

But when men were men, batters expected to be knocked down, and they might retaliate in a more devastating way.

Billy Herman, the Hall of Fame second baseman, once recalled a game at Wrigley Field back in 1942 when the Chicago Cubs—who had traded him to Brooklyn—went hunting for his helmetless Dodger head.

"Jimmy Wilson, who had managed the Cubs, didn't like me. We're playing in Chicago one day and we had all the beanball things going. We were doing most of the beanballing because they had a catcher named Hernandez and a pitcher named Hi Bithorn who didn't like to throw at anybody. Wilson's trying to get us knocked down, and they won't do it.

"So finally I come up to the plate, and he stops the game and takes his catcher and pitcher out. He puts in a new catcher, Clyde McCullough, and a pitcher named Paul Erickson, a big, hard-throwing guy.

"Of course, I'm friendly with most of the guys on the Cubs, and McCullough said, 'You know what this move's all about, don't you?'

"I said, 'Sure, I know.' I knew I was gonna get knocked down. I didn't expect it three times in a row, but Erickson threw three balls right behind my head.

"For some reason, Durocher let me hit three-and-nothing. And I hit one out on Waveland Avenue on the fourth pitch."

Four decades later, helmets were in and knockdown pitches were decidedly out, so far as batters and umpires were concerned.

And so, the question of the day: Was baseball a game for men or for sissies?

Billy Martin didn't like the response he'd get.

The Yankees' John Candelaria wasn't spitting on the ball or scuffing it and he wasn't putting pine tar on his hands. He certainly was not slitting his sleeves. But he most definitely was testing the umpire with a tactic sure to raise a ruckus.

To the Yanks' left-hander, it was a brushback pitch. To the ump, it was target-shooting.

Ever since Connie Mack was a pup, batters have been

crowding the plate while pitchers have been throwing inside to keep the hitters from digging in.

Where to draw the line?

The Yanks were playing the Brewers at Yankee Stadium in mid-April 1988. The season was only two weeks old, but Candelaria had seen enough baseballs rocket over the fence that afternoon to provide his quota through Memorial Day.

In the fourth inning, Milwaukee's Joey Meyer hit his first major league homer. In the fifth, Robin Yount slugged a two-run drive and then the next batter, Rob Deer, hit a bases-empty blow.

That brought Brewer catcher Bill Schroeder to the plate. Schroeder would never be confused with the likes of Roy Campanella, Mickey Cochrane or Gabby Hartnett. He wasn't even Milwaukee's No. 1 catcher, since he couldn't beat B. J. Surhoff out of the job.

But Candelaria—having given up three homers, two of them moments before—took no chances. On the 1–0 pitch, he threw the ball more than a tad inside. It hit Schroeder on the upper back.

Home-plate Umpire Drew Coble was convinced that Candelaria hadn't suddenly lost his control. He accused the pitcher of deliberately throwing at the hitter.

ON THE MOUND

What Could Coble Do to Candelaria?

The rule-makers had decided to get tougher on pitchers taking aim at batters. Candelaria would be an early victim of the crackdown.

In previous seasons, when an umpire felt that a pitcher was intentionally throwing at a hitter, he had to start with a warning. The pitcher and his manager—as well as the opposing manager—would be told that another knock-down pitch, from either team, would mean immediate expulsion of the pitcher. (The umpire could also issue official warnings before a game or prior to any knockdowns during a game if he sensed that hostilities were impending.)

Under the old rule, one side could throw a free knock-down pitch. It was only the retaliation that would bring an ejection.

But when the 1988 season began, the umpire was given a choice of punishments.

He could still start out with a warning, but he could also get as nasty as the pitcher. The ump now had the power to immediately eject the pitcher—and his manager as well— for the first instance of head-hunting.

Candelaria had merely given Schroeder a backache. But Coble, invoking the new rule, threw him out of the game. (The ump let Martin stick around, but the Yankee manager would show little gratitude.)

The Yanks lost the game, 6–3. Afterward, Candelaria would deny having had evil intentions.

"I was trying to pitch him in," he insisted. "They were

diving over the plate and they had the wind at their backs all day. I didn't want to hit the guy."

Now Martin took to philosophizing over the state of the baseball world.

"I don't know what this game is coming to when they throw somebody out like that," he lamented. "What if they'd hit three singles in a row and then he hit the guy? You can't guess what the pitcher is thinking."

"I thought we were supposed to play like men, play aggressive," said Martin. "They're making a sissy game out of it."

Coble took a different view.

"He almost hit the guy on the head," the ump said of Candelaria. "They'd just hit a home run [actually two homers] and he ain't got that bad control."

Coble rejected Martin's view of baseball life, but the umpire's eloquent rejoinder may have brought reassurance for Billy. So long as umps speak this way, baseball ain't likely to succumb to the sissies.

Philadelphia's Baker Bowl seemed designed to drive a pitcher mad. A small mistake to a left-handed batter would mean disaster—a tattooing of the ridiculously close right-field fence or a drive over it and out of sight.

When the 1925 season got under way, things were a tiny

bit easier for Phillie pitchers: The fence at the decrepit wooden bandbox was moved back exactly one foot. Now it was all of 280.5 feet down the line in right to a 40-foot-high tin wall.

It's no wonder Phils pitcher Bill Hubbell was the model of cowardice.

Bill was no relation to the future Hall of Fame pitcher Carl Hubbell—not in terms of family and certainly not in performance. He would win 40 games and lose 63 over his seven-year career in the majors.

One afternoon during the '25 season, the right-hander tried to give an intentional walk to a Cincinnati Reds batter with runners on second and third. But he didn't get one of his pitches far enough out of the strike zone and he was clubbed for a game-winning hit.

The next day, Hubbell was on the mound again, and once more the Reds had men on second and third. The Philadelphia manager, Art Fletcher, ordered another intentional walk. But hardly trusting his pitcher in view of the previous afternoon's debacle, Fletcher came up with a novel tactic.

He told Hubbell to deliver his pitches far from the batter's box. What the pitcher did was throw the ball four times to his first baseman, Walter Holke, who was nowhere near any of the runners.

YOU BE THE UMPIRE!

Did Hubbell Give a Legitimate Intentional Walk?

Much pleased with his ingenuity, Manager Fletcher came out of his dugout, waving a rule book as soon as the fourth "pitch" was thrown. He showed the umpires an obscure rule requiring them to call a "ball" any time a pitcher threw to a base where there was no runner. So Hubbell, having thrown four extremely wide but technically sufficient balls, got his intentional walk without risking another freakish hit.

But the loophole was quickly closed. The next day, a telegram arrived from National League headquarters ordering the Phils not to try the trick again.

A formal change in the rule was eventually made. Now, if a pitcher, while touching the rubber, throws or even feints a throw to an unoccupied base, it's a balk.

On the final day of the 1959 season, a reliever named Humberto Robinson, facing the Milwaukee Braves at County Stadium, threw over to first base in the seventh inning to keep Eddie Mathews close to the bag. The toss greatly surprised Robinson's first baseman, Ed Bouchee, since Mathews was 90 feet away. Moments earlier, he had gone down to second on a passed ball. Robinson had simply forgotten about that little mishap. A balk was called, allowing Mathews to take third base and sending John De-Merit, the runner on third, across the plate.

Humberto Robinson had certainly never heard of the pitcher whose ruse inspired the rule change that brought unpleasant consequences for him three decades later. But Robinson and Bill Hubbell had something in common.

ON THE MOUND

Both wore the uniform of the Philadelphia Phillies. Throwing to an unoccupied base seemed to run in the Phils' family.

It was Wee Willie vs. the Sultan of Swat.

The scene was Sportsman's Park in St. Louis, where the New York Yankees were on their way to an unprecedented feat. Never before had a team swept two consecutive World Series. Now, after beating the Pittsburgh Pirates 4 games to 0 in the 1927 Series, the Yanks had defeated the Cards in the first three games of the '28 Series.

On the mound for St. Louis in Game 4 was Bill Sherdel, a nifty pitcher with a less than imposing physique. He was five feet ten inches and 160 pounds. Not exactly a shrimp, but the press called him "Wee Willie."

The left-hander had won 21 games that season, but now he was up against the mightiest figure of them all.

He'd tried his curveball on Babe Ruth back at the start of the fourth inning, then watched the baseball zoom out of the ballpark.

In the seventh inning, with the Cardinals leading, 2–1, Ruth came to the plate again with one down and nobody on base. Sherdel managed to get an edge, putting two slow curves over for strikes.

After the second pitch went past him, Ruth turned for a

bit of socializing with the Cardinal catcher, "exchanging quips and bright repartee with Earl Smith," as one press account would put it.

Perhaps Ruth was surprised to find Smith behind the plate, since the Cards had used Jimmy Wilson as their starting catcher for nearly every game since June. But after losing the first three games of the Series, St. Louis Manager Bill McKechnie shook up his lineup, inserting Smith for Wilson.

Perhaps Smith was good at small talk, one of his tasks being to divert Ruth's attention.

Whatever the circumstances of this little chat, Sherdel suddenly saw an easy way to get rid of Ruth.

As soon as Smith threw the ball back to him, Sherdel delivered pitch No. 3, putting it across the middle of the plate without a windup. Ruth was still in the batter's box, but he never got a glimpse of the baseball.

Should Ruth Be Called Out on Strikes?

The only thing out of there would be the ball itself. Three pitches later, it would be sailing over the right-field roof for Ruth's second homer of the game.

Home-plate Umpire Cy Pfirman ruled that Sherdel had delivered an illegal "quick pitch." It was a "do-over" with the count remaining 0 balls and 2 strikes.

The ump is supposed to call a "quick pitch" when the ball is delivered "before the batter is reasonably set in the batter's box."

ON THE MOUND

The rule book calls baseball's version of football's no-huddle offense "dangerous," and it's not hard to see why. If the ball is zooming toward the batter's head, he won't be conscious of the threat until he's lying in the dirt, and by then he may not be conscious at all. On a less violent note, the maneuver creates an unfair contest between pitcher and hitter.

Under the current rules, when there are runners on base, the pitcher is charged with a balk if he delivers a "quick pitch." With nobody on base, it's called a ball. But Pfirman simply ruled Sherdel's hurry-up maneuver "no pitch."

Sherdel and his teammates surrounded Pfirman in hot protest. The Cards were especially angry since Sherdel was being deprived of a weapon he might have used during the regular season. Back in 1928, the two leagues differed on the "quick pitch." Although the National League allowed it, the American League didn't, and its view prevailed in the World Series.

Amid the shouting, Ruth was having a good time. He stood off to the side and mockingly clapped at the Cards' futile arguing.

Moments later, Sherdel went back to the mound. His next two pitches were outside. The 2–2 delivery was a slow curve, again a bit off the plate. With an easy swing Ruth lifted the baseball high and far. It cleared the roof of the right-field pavilion and was last seen heading for Grand Avenue.

Ruth trotted around the bases in all his glory, throwing a mock salute to the jeering fans in the left-field bleachers.

YOU BE THE UMPIRE!

It was the beginning of the end for the too-clever Wee Willie Sherdel. The next batter was Lou Gehrig, and he, too, slammed a home run. By time the inning was over, the Yanks had scored four times to take a 5–2 lead.

In the eighth inning Ruth hit his third home run of the game, connecting off Grover Cleveland Alexander. And the Babe finished things off with a flourish. The fans out in left field had been showering him with pop bottles. What better way to quiet them for good than to snare the final out on a terrific catch. And that's just what Ruth did. After a long run, he made a one-handed grab of Frankie Frisch's fly ball to cap the Yankees' 7–3 triumph and a four-game sweep of the Series.

When the game ended, "enough police to form a Mexican regiment"—as the Associated Press put it—stood guard outside the umpires' dressing room to protect them from overzealous Cardinal fans.

In the Yankee dressing room, it was a wild scene, the players shouting triumphantly and then breaking into "The Sidewalks of New York."

Finally, someone yelled, "Ruth for President!" A truly balanced ticket might have matched his brawn with someone else's quick wits. But there were no calls for Wee Willie Sherdel as a running mate.

ON THE MOUND

Their pitching styles and their personalities were in sharp contrast. Dizzy Dean rode a fastball and a folksy arrogance to fame. Carl Hubbell had a wonderful screwball but was otherwise a straight arrow.

One Wednesday afternoon in May 1937, they faced each other when the Cardinals took on the Giants at Sportsman's Park before a remarkable weekday turnout of 26,399.

For Dean, it was just another day to show off his stuff. But Hubbell was seeking his twenty-second consecutive victory in a streak going back to the previous July.

They went to the top of the sixth inning with the Cards leading by 1–0 on Joe Medwick's homer. Burgess Whitehead, the Giant second baseman, opened with a single and was sacrificed to second by Hubbell. The next batter was shortstop Dick Bartell. Dean brought his arms down as he got ready in the set position, but he half turned toward second base and then, continuing his motion without a pause, delivered the ball.

Bartell lifted an easy fly to Medwick in left. But seconds later, the Giant batter would return to the plate for another shot at Dean.

YOU BE THE UMPIRE!

What Had Dizzy Done Wrong?

At issue was the most troublesome split second in baseball, the instant when the pitcher—in the set position as opposed to the full windup—is required to pause before firing away.

If the pitcher doesn't pause, it's a balk—an "illegal act" with somebody on base that results in all runners being awarded the next bag. That's what Umpire George Barr called on Dean.

The balk rules (there are thirteen ways in which a pitcher can balk) are aimed at preventing pitchers from deceiving runners, thereby cutting down their chances to steal a base or making them dead ducks on pickoff throws.

When a pitcher fails to stop his set-position motion for an instant—à la Dizzy Dean—the runner cannot risk taking a decent lead.

Dean argued furiously over the balk call, but to no avail. Whitehead, the runner on second, was ordered to take third base and the delivery was ruled "no pitch."

Bartell made the most of his second chance. Now he hit a liner to right field that Pepper Martin dropped as Whitehead scored. A couple of hits followed the "do-over" and by time the inning ended, the Giants had a 3–1 lead.

Soon Dean turned to head-hunting to vent his anger. He couldn't deck the ump so he went after more accessible targets. Hitter after Giant hitter bit the dust.

By the ninth inning the Giants decided they'd had enough, even by the liberal beanballing standards of the era. When center fielder Jimmy Ripple was put on the seat

ON THE MOUND

of his pants, he nodded toward the New York dugout—the time for retaliation had come.

Moments later Ripple sent a sharp bunt to the right side. Second baseman Jimmy Brown picked the ball up and got set to toss it to first baseman Johnny Mize. But now Dean decided to get involved, just as Ripple had hoped he would. He ran over to the baseline to block Ripple's path.

Dean and Ripple collided and then the punches began to fly. Both benches emptied for a wonderful melee and, amid the tangle of bodies, the two catchers—Mickey Owen of the Cards and Gus Mancuso of the Giants—got into a brawl of their own.

Order was eventually restored by the three umpires and park policemen. Then Dean, who strangely had not been ejected, really got serious about his target-shooting. He hit the next batter, Johnny McCarthy, the first Giant he had actually plunked.

Hubbell was about the only player who'd avoided the brawl. He would go on to more serious matters, like his twenty-third straight triumph, which he soon nailed down in the Giants' 4–1 victory.

The rule requiring a pause in the set position has rarely led to violent outbursts like Dean's. But every once in a while, baseball officialdom decides to enforce it strictly, and then there's trouble.

Until 1950, the pitcher merely had to come to a "stop" in his motion. But then the rule was changed to require a pause of "one full second."

The umpires had no stopwatches, so the stricter rule

wasn't enforced all that often. But in the winter following the 1962 season, Dodger Manager Walter Alston pushed for living up to the letter of the law. Since the Dodgers relied on speed—Maury Wills had stolen a record 104 bases in '62—anything that could shackle the pitchers with runners on base would be a wonderful gift for them.

Alston asked National League President Warren Giles to enforce the "one-second" rule, and Giles ordered his umpires to do so.

It was a fiasco. The major league record for balks in a single season had been 76, but by the first week of May '63, a total of 96 had been called in the National League. (The American League was, as usual, paying little attention to the balk rule. Only eight balks had been called there.)

Finally, the screams of the other National League teams outweighed the Dodgers' argument. Embarrassed by the balk mania, Commissioner Ford Frick called Giles and American League President Joe Cronin together. When the meeting ended, the "one-second" rule was still on the books but it would once again be ignored. The National League agreed to go back to simply making sure that a pitcher came to some sort of stop in his set position.

The "one-second" requirement was eventually thrown out and replaced by a directive that pitchers merely come to "a complete stop." But twenty-five years later, the arguing would begin all over again.

In 1988, the balk rule was revised once more, this time on a one-year trial basis. Now the pitcher had to come to a "complete and discernible stop."

ON THE MOUND

Discernible meant *disaster* so far as baseball's image would go.

A total of 924 balks would be called during 1988 in comparison with 356 the previous season.

As in 1963, it seemed that the balk orgy stemmed from complaints by a ball club geared toward speed.

During the 1987 World Series, Cardinal Manager Whitey Herzog had complained that the Minnesota Twins' Bert Blyleven wasn't coming to a stop with runners on base. Like the Dodgers of '62, the Cardinals looked at base stealing as a big weapon, so they needed to handcuff the pitchers.

Herzog would become the villain in the 1988 balkathon.

When the California Angels' DeWayne Buice was called for a balk with the bases loaded one day during the '88 season, his manager, Marcel Lachemann, knew where to place the blame.

"They're going to make some rules because that little white-haired bleep in the National League moaned," Lachemann was quoted as saying. (He may not have actually used the word *bleep*.)

The following December, the experimental change in the balk ruling was dropped. No longer would a pitcher's stop have to be "discernible."

But if a stop is not discernible, how can the umpire tell that it actually happened? Don't look to the rule book for the answer.

YOU BE THE UMPIRE!

Heat prostration at Candlestick Park?

It happened at an All-Star Game in 1961 when a freakish weather system stagnated over San Francisco, sending the temperature soaring to eighty-five degrees. While not exactly tropical, that was plenty high for the Bay Area. Before the game had ended, ninety-five fans were felled.

But some of them may have succumbed to boredom. The game had moved along uneventfully for eight innings with the National League holding a 3–1 lead.

Then the inevitable struck—the notorious Candlestick winds finally arrived. The infield dirt was sent swirling and the fans' red, yellow and blue Chinese sun hats began to fly as well. Many in the crowd of 44,115 headed for the exits.

The early departures would be sorry. For the entertainment was just beginning.

The American League rallied for a run in the top of the ninth with one out, and then the San Francisco Giants' Stu Miller came in to pitch with Al Kaline on second base and Roger Maris on first.

Miller had three kinds of pitches: slow, slower and slowest. The 158-pound right-hander would hardly blow anyone away.

What happened next was just the reverse: The Candlestick wind blew him away.

As Miller went into his motion, facing Rocky Colavito, a gust picked him up and deposited him two feet south of the pitching rubber. He managed to hang on to the baseball but never delivered it.

What Happens to Kaline and Maris?

The runners took a ninety-foot stroll—they were awarded an extra base.

Home-plate Umpire Stan Landes may have had sympathy for Miller's plight, but he nonetheless did his duty. Miller had broken the first of the thirteen commandments in the balk regulations. It's a balk when the pitcher, while on the rubber, "makes any motion naturally associated with his pitch and fails to make such delivery."

Miller's plan to deliver the pitch was gone with the wind, so Landes waved Kaline to third base and Maris to second.

The chaos was, however, only beginning.

Moments later, third baseman Ken Boyer botched a grounder hit by Colavito as Kaline scored to tie the game. Miller's catcher, Smoky Burgess, then dropped a pop foul hit by Tony Kubek. Miller eventually struck Kubek out, but his teammates would soon let him down for a third time. Second baseman Don Zimmer pulled first baseman Bill White off the bag with his throw on a ground ball hit by Yogi Berra.

Now the bases were loaded, but Miller finally retired the side and the game went to extra innings. In the top of the tenth, there was more bad luck for Miller. After Nelson Fox walked, Boyer made another error, throwing Kaline's grounder into right field—with help from the wind—as Fox scored.

But in the bottom of the inning, the wind would do its bit for the National League, sending a knuckleball from American League reliever Hoyt Wilhelm floating into Frank Robinson. Another Wilhelm knuckler would go astray on a passed ball and the National League would come up with a pair of hits. When the dust settled, the Nationals had scored twice for a 5–4 victory. Miller, despite his travails, became the winning pitcher.

On July 10, 1984, the All-Star Game returned to Candlestick Park. Two former Giant pitchers were guests of honor for the opening ceremonies.

One celebrity was Carl Hubbell, who, at an All-Star Game in the Polo Grounds fifty years earlier, had stunned the baseball world with consecutive strikeouts of Babe Ruth, Lou Gehrig, Jimmie Foxx, Al Simmons and Joe Cronin, all future Hall of Famers.

The other VIP was the man who would be remembered for the All-Star Game pitch that wasn't: little Stu Miller.

It was a pitching duel of refugees from Mexican baseball when the New York Giants played the St. Louis Cardinals at Sportsman's Park on a Saturday afternoon in August 1949.

The starting pitchers, Adrian Zabala of the Giants and

ON THE MOUND

Max Lanier of the Cards, had been barred from organized baseball in 1946 by Commissioner Happy Chandler for deserting to the Mexican League, an outlaw circuit enticing big leaguers with what passed for big money in those days. But by '49, all the renegades had been restored to baseball's good graces, and now two of them were facing each other.

Zabala, a thirty-two-year-old lefty from Cuba, got into trouble quickly when Red Schoendienst, the Cardinal second baseman, doubled with one down. Then Nippy Jones, the first baseman and cleanup man, clubbed a pitch into the left-field bleachers with two men out.

Jones connected a second or two after Zabala had violated pitching protocol by failing to pause in the set position. As Zabala threw the pitch that became a home-run ball, Bill Stewart, the umpire at first base, called a balk.

Did Jones's Homer Count?

It didn't then, but it would now.

When the ball landed in the grandstand, a roar went up from the crowd of 28,193. But the cheers turned to jeers when the confused fans saw Schoendienst being waved back to second and Jones instructed to pick up his bat again. An announcement over the public-address system moments later explained that a balk had been called and so the pitch didn't count.

Zabala had benefited from his own violation of the rules.

Instead of giving up two runs, he eventually got out of the inning without being scored upon.

He went on to pitch a six-hitter in a 3–1 complete-game victory despite committing two more balks, setting what was then a National League record for most balks in a game. (It was to be the fourth and final victory of his big league career—two wins in '45 for the Giants, another two in '49.)

The Cardinals were in first place that weekend in a tight race with the Dodgers. But when the season ended, they were in second—a single game behind Brooklyn. Their homer that was called back by a balk might have made the difference.

But now a pitcher can't luck out the way Zabala did. In 1953, a rule change gave the team at bat the option of negating a balk if the batter reached base and the runner or runners advanced at least one bag.

The Detroit Tigers took advantage of the new rule in a game against the Orioles in 1957. When Charlie Maxwell singled in a run off a balk delivery by Baltimore's Connie Johnson, there was no "do-over."

But matters got more complicated in a Yanks–Blue Jays game at Yankee Stadium in April 1977.

Umpire Dave Phillips called a fourth-inning balk against Toronto's Jerry Garvin just as he pitched to Lou Piniella with two out and Jim Wynn on third base. Piniella swung anyway and hit a liner that bounced out of the center fielder's glove. He made it to second base but Wynn didn't bother to run home since he'd seen the balk call and figured he had a free pass to the plate.

ON THE MOUND

Where Should Piniella and Wynn Wind Up?

The Yanks had a four-game losing streak going and a Billy-vs.-George dispute brewing that day. Billy Martin, having received a suggestion from George Steinbrenner as to what his batting order should be, met with the boss before the game to thrash out just who was running the team on the field. Then Steinbrenner met with the players, telling them everything was fine between owner and manager. After that, Steinbrenner called in the reporters to tell them "if anybody says I've been on Billy Martin's butt, he's a liar."

So when the game began, Martin could hardly have been in the best of moods, Steinbrenner's assurances notwithstanding. By the fourth inning, he was truly in ill-temper.

After deliberating awhile over the balk call, the umps ordered Piniella back to home plate. Because Wynn had not advanced one base on Piniella's double, the balk went into effect and the hit was nullified. Now Wynn was waved home, but Piniella was told to bat again.

Martin argued that not only should Wynn have been allowed to score, but that Piniella should have stayed on second base.

When the umpires held firm, Martin protested the game. The Yanks went on to lose it, 8–3, and Martin would lose the protest as well. The rule book simply wasn't on his side.

Martin would lead the Yankees to a World Series victory

that year. But 94 games into the 1978 season, Billy was out. George had finally landed on his butt.

He was a native of Indiana but he would become part of the Flatbush vernacular—the man they called "Oisk."

Carl Erskine would be a favorite of Dodger fans during the 1950s, his overhand curveball helping keep Brooklyn atop the National League. But as a rookie back in 1948, he was certainly dispensable. One August day at Forbes Field, Manager Burt Shotton yanked Erskine from a game before he had a chance to show what he could do.

The Dodgers and Pittsburgh Pirates had gone into the bottom of the ninth with Brooklyn leading by 11–6, but reliever Hugh Casey was being hammered. Three runs crossed and the Pirates had Ed Fitzgerald on first base and Frank Gustine on third with two out.

Now Shotton summoned Erskine to face Eddie Bockman, who was batting for pitcher Forrest Main. The count went to 3 balls and 1 strike, but then the manager decided to make another move. He took Erskine out and brought Hank Behrman in. Behrman got Bockman to hit a grounder to Pee Wee Reese, and the Dodgers seemingly had emerged with an 11–9 victory.

ON THE MOUND

Was Bockman Legally Retired?

An old-timer named James Long was doing publicity work for the Pirates in those days. A former sportswriter, Long had memories of baseball going as far back as the 1890s. But that afternoon he remembered something far more significant for Pittsburgh.

The rule book says that unless a pitcher suffers an immediate injury, he must complete an encounter with one batter before he can be removed. (The rare exception: If a reliever gets out of an inning because a runner is picked off or caught stealing while he's facing his first batter, he doesn't have to begin the next inning.)

Erskine did not finish off his batter and he didn't qualify for any exceptions to the rule.

Nobody on the field had noticed the oversight. Dodger Manager Shotton, Pirate Manager Billy Meyer and the three umpires were, in effect, all asleep.

But Long wasn't, and he communicated his discovery to Meyer in the clubhouse. The manager protested to league headquarters.

Ford Frick, the National League president, upheld the protest and ordered that the game be resumed from the point at which Erskine had departed. And Erskine would have to return to the mound.

The Dodgers and Pirates had no more games left in Pittsburgh that season. So the disputed game—played on August 25—would be finished off before a regularly scheduled game at Ebbets Field.

The teams returned on September 21 with the same

YOU BE THE UMPIRE!

lineups except at third base, where Tommy Brown replaced an ailing Billy Cox for the Dodgers, a substitution that would loom large. (Brown's claim to fame was his appearance in a big league lineup at the age of sixteen years and seven months back in 1944 when everyone was scrambling for warm bodies untouched by the military. He'd done nothing very special since then.)

Erskine returned to the mound in the situation from which he had illegally departed it—runners on first and third, two out, a 3–1 count on Eddie Bockman, and the Dodgers leading by 11–9.

He walked the bases loaded on the next pitch. Now Burt Shotton repeated what he had done the first time—he summoned Hank Behrman. This time, instead of pitching to Bockman, Behrman faced the following batter, Stan Rojek, the Pirate shortstop. He fell behind by 3–0, then came in with two strikes. On the next pitch, Rojek hit a hard grounder between third and short. Brown got his glove on the ball, but it bounded away into short center field. Rojek wound up with a fluke double and all three runners came home—finishing off a six-run inning—for a 12–11 Pirate victory. The resumption took all of three minutes, but when it was over, Pittsburgh had ended a three-game losing streak.

A protest like this one will not, however, be lodged again. A rule adopted in 1957 states that if a pitcher is brought in illegally and nobody notices the oversight, the reliever becomes a proper pitcher once he makes his first delivery.

Erskine's abortive appearance at Forbes Field did, at

least, outlast the major league debut of Rube Marquard. Having been bought by the New York Giants for $11,000—the heftiest purchase price that had ever been paid for a minor leaguer—Marquard was the center of attention at the Polo Grounds when he was summoned by John McGraw in the fifth inning of a game on September 18, 1908, against the Cardinals. But after a few warm-up pitches, Marquard took his seat on the bench once again. Luther (Dummy) Taylor—he was a deaf-mute and nicknames in those days were not chosen for their sensitivity—was brought in as the real relief pitcher. McGraw had simply been using Marquard to stall so Taylor would have more time to get ready. (The Giants weren't cheating. The "one-batter" rule was not in the books back then.) Marquard would, however, have his moments in the sun. He got into only one game that season, but would win 201 games over an eighteen-year career.

In September 1971, a right-handed pitcher named Larry Yount would make a big league debut that equaled Marquard's for pitches thrown. The twenty-one-year-old Yount was brought in by the Houston Astros in the ninth inning against the Atlanta Braves. But as Yount took his warm-up tosses, he felt pain in his elbow, so he was removed by Manager Harry Walker without throwing a pitch.

Yount had experienced some stiffness before taking the mound but, he recalled long afterward, "I wasn't going to turn down a chance to show them what I could do. I thought I may never get another opportunity."

He never did. Yount would return to the minors and stay there until retiring in 1976.

YOU BE THE UMPIRE!

Three years after the debut that wasn't, Larry Yount's younger brother, Robin, would break in with Milwaukee and he would roll up impressive statistics over a long career as an infielder and outfielder. Larry's line in the record books would show one game "pitched"—since he'd appeared in the box score—and then a string of zeroes. He's presumably the only pitcher in major league history who never threw a single pitch.

 The Cardinals' Billy Muffett ran out of time before he could get started.

The Cards were playing the Phillies in the second game of a Sunday doubleheader at Shibe Park on June 29, 1958. It was the eighth inning, and the Phils, trailing by 4–2, had runners on first and third with one out. Muffett was called in to relieve Morrie Martin. But before he threw his first pitch, the Pennsylvania Sunday curfew took effect. (No game could go beyond 6:00 P.M.) The game was suspended and then resumed the following July 29. When the teams took the field again, the Cardinals sent Jim Brosnan to the mound, replacing Muffett.

ON THE MOUND

Should Muffett Have Been Brought Back to Finish Facing One Batter?

When a game is suspended, so is the rule requiring that a pitcher face at least one hitter before he is taken out. "Any player may be replaced by a player who had not been in the game prior to the suspension," says the rule book. Any player means any pitcher as well.

Muffett was sent down to Omaha of the American Association after that suspended game, but he was recalled a few days before it was to be completed. Nevertheless, the Cards went with Brosnan instead, and he got a perfectly legal "save" in a 4–3 victory that took the Cards a month to complete.

Suspended games can bring odd statistics.

On July 14, 1991, Kip Gross was the losing pitcher in two games played 1,100 miles apart.

Gross was the starter and loser when the Reds were beaten by the Pirates, 10–6, in Cincinnati. The previous May 15, he had pitched for Nashville in an American Association game against Denver that was suspended by rain. When that game was completed in Denver the same day as the Reds-Pirates game, Gross became the losing pitcher there as well even though he was one-third of a continent away.

"Hey, that's a tough day," Gross observed.

Back in June, when he was in the minors, Gross's Nashville apartment was robbed. Two days after that, he was among several players held up while walking back to their hotel after a game in Richmond.

YOU BE THE UMPIRE!

Whether he was on the field or off it, that was a lost summer for Kip Gross.

When the California Angels went to spring training in March 1988, Cookie Rojas held a modest position in their so-called brain trust. He was about to enter his seventh year as a scout, and meanwhile he busied himself by helping Angel infielders with their techniques. Then Gene Mauch, suffering from chronic bronchitis, suddenly quit as manager. He recommended Rojas to succeed him, and Cookie got the job.

Rojas had played sixteen seasons in the majors as an infielder, but his managerial experience was limited to a few winters in Caribbean baseball. Now he would be called upon to replace one of the game's most astute strategists.

By time the '88 season headed into its final week, Rojas's Angels were in fourth place, a few games below the .500 mark. But the new manager had presumably sharpened his baseball wisdom over the course of the summer, and when California played the Minnesota Twins on the evening of September 23 at Anaheim Stadium, the strategic wheels were indeed turning.

In the seventh inning, Rojas sent his pitching coach, Marcel Lachemann, out to the mound for a conference with reliever Rich Monteleone. Moments later, deciding that Monteleone needed even more guidance, Rojas himself strolled out for a chat.

What Was Monteleone's Immediate Fate?

Rojas had no desire to remove Monteleone—he simply wanted to convey some words of wisdom. But as soon as the manager arrived at the mound, the umps sent the pitcher to the showers.

In an effort to keep games moving along, the rule book limits visits to the mound by a manager or coach, decreeing that "a second trip to the same pitcher in the same inning will cause this pitcher's automatic removal."

Rojas had visited Monteleone only once during the inning. But a manager can't get around the rule by having a coach make the other trip.

Had Rojas been trying to skirt the rules? Not at all. So why had he gone to the mound when the consequence was a pitching change he didn't want to make?

"It just slipped my mind," the embarrassed manager admitted afterward.

The Angels lost the game—their fourth straight defeat —and the newspapers were hardly charitable despite Rojas's confession.

The headlines read:

COOKIE LOSES COUNT, ANGELS LOSE GAME.

MENTAL LAPSE MANAGES TO HIT ANGELS WITH 6–2 LOSS TO TWINS.

YOU BE THE UMPIRE!

ONCE AGAIN, ROJAS KEEPS THEM OFF BALANCE AS TWINS GET PAST CALIFORNIA.

The morning after the game, Angel General Manager Mike Port called Rojas into his office. For the second time in under twenty-four hours, the manager would be involved in a change he had no desire to see carried out. This time, it was Rojas himself who was a goner—the Angels fired him.

3

AT THE PLATE

The feats of the great Negro leagues slugger Josh Gibson are the stuff of legend.

Batting for the Pittsburgh Crawfords one day at Forbes Field in the early 1930s, Gibson hit a ball that traveled so high and far that nobody saw it descend. The umpires watched the heavens for a while, then grew tired of waiting for the baseball to come down. So they called it a home run.

The following day, the Crawfords moved on for a game in Philadelphia. Something had been following them. The center fielder for the other team suddenly saw a ball emerging from the clouds. He caught it, and the umpire had no doubts about what to do next with Gibson.

"Yer out—yesterday in Pittsburgh," he cried.

Tall tales aside, even the most fabulous of hitters will be frustrated most of the time. Encountering a spinning baseball approaching at speeds exceeding ninety miles an hour, the batter will fail on at least two of every three trips to the plate.

And just as the rule book keeps a close watch on the pitcher, so, too, does it see that the batter will not dominate baseball's central confrontation.

There aren't too many things a hitter is allowed to do to his bat except swing it. He can't drive nails into the wood to make it harder, he can't flatten out one side, and—as a certain batter for the Kansas City Royals once found out—not too heavy on the pine tar, please.

The hitter had better stay in the batter's box when he does swing. Hank Aaron once had a home run nullified because he crossed the front line as he moved up on a blooper pitch.

There are fourteen ways in which a batter can be retired. Josh Gibson wasn't the only Negro leagues hero to perform a supernatural feat yet run afoul of the rule book. There's the story about the time James (Cool Papa) Bell hit a scorcher up the middle but had nothing to show for it. Cool Papa could run like the wind. He was so fast that on this occasion he got to second base before his line drive arrived there. He was called out, legend has it, when the ball hit him on the fly.

Rule 6.05 (g)—detailing instance No. 7 among the fourteen-point "yer out of there" rules—says that "a batter is out when his fair ball touches him before touching a fielder."

It could happen. If a batter admires his bunt and then trips over the ball, he goes back to the dugout. A less spectacular occurrence than in the Cool Papa Bell legend, but an out nonetheless.

When a hitter steps out of the box for a prolonged argument with the ump, that, too, can cost him. If he ignores an

AT THE PLATE

order to get back in, the umpire can direct the pitcher to throw the ball for an automatic strike.

One July day during the 1949 season, a rookie outfielder for the Pittsburgh Pirates named Dino Restelli was quite full of himself. When Umpire Larry Goetz called a couple of strikes on him in a game at Forbes Field against the Cardinals, he twice stepped out of the batter's box with great indignation.

Goetz finally had enough of the bickering and told St. Louis pitcher Gerry Staley to deliver the ball while Restelli continued to grouse. Staley lobbed the baseball to the plate. Suddenly, Restelli jumped back in and clobbered the ball. He sent a two-run double to left field that won the game.

A lesson for the batter: Even when the umpire is riled, a little initiative can rule the day.

The fans idolized him as "Big Bill." The founder of *The Sporting News,* Al Spink, would remember him as "Ty Cobb enlarged, fully as great in speed, batting skill and base running."

In the Chicago of the 1890s, Bill Lange was a baseball hero. He was colorful, he was aggressive, and he'd even carve a niche in the game's folklore. An oft-told story had Lange running through an outfield fence to catch a baseball. It never happened, but Bernard Malamud borrowed the tale for an episode in *The Natural.*

YOU BE THE UMPIRE!

On the afternoon of August 22, 1894, the White Stockings' wonderful outfielder was, however, hardly himself. He had been struck out twice at the Polo Grounds by the Giants' Jouett Meekin. By the eighth inning, he was ready to try anything for a change of luck.

The manager of the Madison Square Theatre in Manhattan, a fellow named Frank McKee, evidently had his baseball heart in Chicago. He had bestowed a rather large gift on Jimmy Ryan, one of Lange's fellow outfielders: a bat that measured five feet ten inches in length and five inches in diameter at its thickest part.

Lange figured it was he who needed the extra lumber if he was ever going to make contact that particular afternoon. And so he arrived at the plate carrying the super bat.

Was Lange's Bat Too Big for the Rule Book?

At baseball's dawn, back in the 1860s, there was no limit on the length of a bat. But by the 1890s, a five-foot-ten-inch bat was as illegal as it would be today.

The length of a bat was limited then—as it is now—to forty-two inches.

But Lange did get to wield the oversized present. He asked Umpire John McQuaid to let him have one shot with it, and since the Giants were six runs ahead at the time, they didn't object. McQuaid gave his permission, and Lange—at six feet one and a half inches only slightly bigger than his bat—stepped to the plate amid great hilarity in the crowd.

All he could manage, however, was an easy grounder to Jack Doyle, the Giants' first baseman. But he did get on base when Doyle, perhaps doubled over with laughter, fumbled the ball.

The next batter, Charlie Irwin, decided that he, too, wanted to use the big bat. But John Montgomery Ward, the Giants' manager, wasn't taking any chances with the White Stockings' luck turning for the better. He finally protested, and Umpire McQuaid threw the bat out. Reduced to their regular bats, the White Stockings went on to lose the game, 8–5.

Lange would hit well over .300 every year through 1899, but then he stunned baseball by retiring in his prime. His girlfriend's father had refused to allow her to marry a professional ballplayer. Forced to chose between his love for baseball and the love of his life, Lange opted for the latter.

The marriage would, unfortunately, prove no more successful than his encounter with that superbat. It ended in divorce.

When Edd Roush suffered a fatal heart attack at age ninety-four on March 21, 1988, it was the baseball equivalent of the cowboy who "died with his boots on." The old-time Cincinnati Reds outfielder was at a ballpark when he was stricken. He had gone to Bill Mc-Kechnie Field in Bradenton, Florida, to see the Pittsburgh Pirates play the Texas Rangers in an exhibition game.

Roush happened to be the final surviving ballplayer from the infamous "Black Sox" World Series of 1919. But he had another distinction: He used the heaviest bats and thickest bat handles of any hitter in baseball history.

According to a statistical inventory once conducted by John Hillerich of the "Louisville Slugger" bat company, Roush's forty-eight-ounce bats, with their inch-and-a-quarter handles, were the heftiest ever.

Babe Ruth is generally considered to have wielded the heaviest bats, but Hillerich said that Ruth didn't go beyond forty-two ounces during the regular season. He ordered fifty-ounce bats for spring training, but that was just to give him what passed for exercise in his less than spartan lifestyle.

What Is the Limit on the Weight and Thickness of a Bat?

The weight limit depends on what the batter can lug around. As long as his bat doesn't exceed forty-two inches and is made of solid wood, the hitter doesn't have to worry about exceeding any specific weight.

There is a limit on the bat's thickness, but Roush wasn't close to it. Since 1895, the rules have put the bat's maximum diameter at 2¾ inches.

Roush once claimed that he had never broken a bat.

"I used to order six bats each year," he recalled. "That's

because the clubhouse boy would take two or three and I'd give the rest away after the season."

And he got good use out of his lumber: He hit over .300 for eleven straight seasons.

His secret?

"Didn't swing my head off, just snapped at the ball."

Over an eighteen-year career in the American League, Goose Goslin would amass 2,735 hits and he would ultimately enter the Hall of Fame. So he hardly needed any tricks to gain an edge.

But on opening day of the 1932 season, he came to the plate with a bat designed to befuddle the men in the field. Playing right field for the St. Louis Browns and batting in the number-three slot, Goslin stepped up in the first inning against the Chicago White Sox. But he was promptly asked to step out again by Umpire Harry Geisel. In dispute: his "camouflage" or "zebra" bat, painted with black and white stripes running up and down the lumber.

Was Goslin's Bat Legal?

Goslin argued with the ump for a moment, then put the bat away. He said later he was convinced the bat didn't violate the rules but that he hadn't prolonged his discussion with Geisel because "I'm not in good arguing form yet —too early in the season." (The 18,000 fans at Comiskey Park were no doubt grateful that Goslin hadn't carried on for too long. They were described as "half frozen" on this mid-April day.)

The dispute was sent to Will Harridge, the American League president, who threw the bat out permanently, ruling it was a piece of trickery going beyond good sportsmanship. Using the bat was put in the same category with a pitcher sewing a white webbing into his glove to keep the batter from picking up the baseball as it was delivered.

Goslin's bat was, in fact, designed for more than artistic merit. In masterminding the paint job, Willis Johnson, the Browns' secretary, hoped that the pattern would keep the fielders from immediately locating the flight of the ball when it came off the bat.

The rule book anticipates a ruse like this one, saying that "no colored bat may be used" unless approved by the Rules Committee. (Natural staining—accounting for the light or dark "finish" on a bat—is okay.)

Goslin had a superb day even without his stripes. Settling for the first bat he saw in the dugout, he hit two doubles and a single, drove in one run, and scored another. But it wasn't enough. The White Sox not only won the bat argument but they took the game, 9–2.

One day at Yankee Stadium, when Goslin was playing for the Detroit Tigers, he would be on the receiving end of a bit of deception. This time it was entirely legal.

Yankee pitcher Red Ruffing liked to work the hidden-ball trick with shortstop Frank Crosetti, who would feign handing the baseball to Ruffing after a play while keeping it in his glove.

Many years later, George Selkirk, the man who replaced Babe Ruth in the Yanks' lineup, would remember the stunt:

"We were playing Detroit and we picked Gerald Walker off second base one day. And Goose Goslin told Crosetti, 'You so-and-so, you'll never pick me off with that play. I know what the story is.' So we're playing in New York this day and I'm in right field. And I see Crosetti go in to give Ruffing the ball, and boom, Crosetti put it in his glove and walked back to the shortstop position. Goslin walked off the bag a couple of steps. Crosetti walked in behind him, took the ball out, and he said, 'Hey, Goose, look what I got.' I thought Goslin would kill him."

When the Yanks' Graig Nettles broke his bat swinging one afternoon in a September 1974 game against the Tigers, he got a single. But he presumably wished he'd missed the pitch altogether.

As *The Detroit News* put it: "Nettles stood on first base looking like the bald man whose wig blew away."

Nettles had hit a homer in the first game of that day's doubleheader at Shea Stadium, New York's temporary home during renovation of Yankee Stadium. In the second inning of the nightcap, the Yankee third baseman homered again. The drive would represent all the scoring in New York's 1–0 triumph, but it was Nettles's subsequent at-bat that would prove far more remarkable.

In the fifth inning, he blooped a hit to left field off Woody Fryman. As the baseball flew from home plate, so did the top of Nettles's bat. When Tiger catcher Bill Freehan picked the bat up, he made an interesting discovery. It was packed with cork that had been placed inside after the wood was hollowed out.

Was Nettles Entitled to His Single and to the Home Run He Hit Earlier in the Game?

The single was taken away, but the homer stood.

The rule book says a batter is to be called out when "he uses or attempts to use a bat that, in the umpire's judgment, has been altered or tampered with . . . to improve the distance factor."

One way for a mere mortal of a hitter to temporarily assume Ruthian proportions is "corking" the bat. Although the top of Nettles's bat had been sawed off before the corking began, the orthodox method is simply to drill a hole down through the bat's center, then fill the space with cork and apply paint to cover up the tampering. Because the cork is lighter than the wood it replaces—generally white ash—the hitter can whip the bat more quickly and thereby get greater "pop" on the ball while still wielding the sturdy lumber of a bat designed to be heavier.

AT THE PLATE

The home-plate umpire, Lou DiMuro, called Nettles out when his bat blew its top, exposing the cork.

Nettles's home run a few innings earlier wasn't erased. There was no way for the Tigers to prove that he used the tainted bat to hit that drive. And even assuming he had, it was too late for the umps to do anything about it.

Nettles claimed, in fact, that the homer had been hit with a bat he borrowed from a teammate, Walt Williams, and that he later switched bats.

Where had he gotten the corked bat?

"That was the first time I used it," he insisted. "Some Yankee fan in Chicago gave it to me. He said it would bring me luck. I guess he made it. I've been using Walt Williams's bat the past three days and I picked this one up by mistake. It looked the same and it felt the same. As soon as the end came off, I knew there was something wrong with it."

The fuss died down quickly. But in the summer of 1987, corked-bat allegations were flying like never before when home runs jumped by 22.4 percent over the previous season.

Baseball officials insisted that the balls weren't juiced up, so suspicion fell upon the bats. Commissioner Peter Ueberroth issued a directive allowing a manager to challenge one bat a game. A manager who felt that an opposing hitter might be corking up (or who simply wanted to harass the batter) could have the umpires remove the player's bat.

And so the great X-ray frenzy was born as bats were carted off to radiology labs in the search for cork. The

YOU BE THE UMPIRE!

Mets' Howard Johnson, who was hitting homers way beyond the level he'd been known for, had his bat subjected to X rays twice in two weeks.

No cork was ever found via X rays. But one player did get caught that season. The Houston Astros' Billy Hatcher broke his bat in a game against the Chicago Cubs, and cork was discovered inside it. The National League president, Bart Giamatti, suspended Hatcher for ten days and fined his manager, Hal Lanier, holding him responsible for his players' equipment.

In the midst of all this bickering a belated explanation was offered for Graig Nettles's corking adventure.

Gene Michael, the Cubs' manager in 1987, had been the Yankee shortstop that afternoon back in '74. Now he revealed a secret that another former Yankee—Bill Sudakis, the first baseman that day—had confided to him a week before the fiasco.

"He told me how he had cut about two inches off the top of the bat, drilled down into the bat, filled the hole and then glued the top back on," Michaels recalled.

"I said, 'You can't keep the top on. The end has to fly off when he hits the ball.'

"He said, 'No, it'll never come off. I put it back on with Elmer's glue.'

"About a week later, Nettles hits the ball off the end of the bat and bloops a single and the end comes off."

AT THE PLATE

Ted Simmons was around the major leagues long enough to learn a ton of tricks. He played for twenty-one seasons, breaking in as a catcher with the St. Louis Cardinals in 1968 and hanging on until 1988, when he wound up his career with the Atlanta Braves.

Beyond preserving his physique for the rigors of catching, Simmons had figured out a way to preserve his bats as well.

In the summer of 1975, he was grooving them—carving indentations along the barrel. The way Simmons would explain it, these lines—created generally with a key or knife—kept the grains farthest from the center of the bat from breaking when he made contact with the ball.

One of Simmons's grooved bats proved sturdy indeed the night of July 21, 1975, when he led off the fourth inning for the Cardinals in a game against the Padres at San Diego. Batting against lefty Brent Strom, Simmons walloped the ball over the left-field fence to give St. Louis a 2–0 lead.

By now the Padres' manager, John McNamara, had seen one crushed ball too many. He'd noticed that many baseballs hit by the Cardinals earlier in the series had cuts in them. "I figured I'd better check some of those bats," he remarked later.

So McNamara asked the umpires to take a good look at Simmons's bat.

YOU BE THE UMPIRE!

Should Simmons's Home Run Have Counted?

After mulling things over for a while, the umpires deprived Simmons of both his bat and his homer, and they called him out.

Simmons had run afoul of the regulation stating "the bat shall be a smooth, rounded stick."

Following the game—a 4–0 St. Louis victory—Simmons said he hadn't known about "the new rule against grooving." He maintained that many players grooved their bats and it "doesn't do anything to make the ball go farther or powerize it. The idea is to keep the bats from fraying."

There was, in fact, no new rule prohibiting grooving, merely an old rule requiring bats to be smooth. But in future years there would be no room for debate. A change in the rule book would specifically outlaw grooved bats on grounds they could—contrary to Simmons's assurances— "improve the distance factor or cause an unusual reaction on the baseball."

The theory is that grooving a bat—like "scoring" the face of a golf club—can impart backspin that will enable a ball to carry farther.

Simmons would, of course, survive quite nicely. He hit a double his next time up in that Padres game and went on to slug 248 homers during his career, most of them presumably coming off bats that were good without being groovy.

AT THE PLATE

 For the ballplayer, it was a moment of pure rage. For the umpire, an instant of terror.

The scene has been shown so many times that the image will long remain vivid: George Brett charges out of the Kansas City Royals' dugout and tears toward Umpire Tim McClelland. Only a headlock applied by the umpiring crew chief, Joe Brinkman, averts calamity.

Brett had just been deprived of a home run in the great pine-tar furor, the grandest baseball dispute since Fred Merkle's "boner" of 1908.

For the first time in baseball history, the team that hit a game-ending homer had lost the game.

It was a Sunday afternoon at Yankee Stadium, July 24, 1983. Brett, one of baseball's premier hitters, had come to bat in the ninth inning against Rich Gossage with the Yankees leading, 4–3, two men out and a man on base. Suddenly, Brett seemed to save the day for the Royals. He drove the ball into the right-field seats to give Kansas City a 5–4 lead, trotted around the bases, then accepted congratulations in the dugout.

But now Yankee Manager Billy Martin walked up to home plate and asked the umpires to examine Brett's bat. It happened to be his favorite, what he called a "seven-grainer." The fewer the grains, the better the wood.

The bat may have been pleasingly short on grains, but it was long on pine tar—at least five inches too long.

Pine tar is applied by batters to give them a better grip.

YOU BE THE UMPIRE!

The rule book says that the bat may be covered with "any substance to improve the grip" but that the material may not extend for more than eighteen inches up from the handle. Any material exceeding that limitation "shall cause the bat to be removed from the game."

Martin said later that he noticed Brett was applying a heavy dose of pine tar when the Yankees were in Kansas City two weeks earlier. He was waiting for the right moment to complain, and what better time than after a home run that seemed about to win a game.

He told the umps that the pine tar appeared to run up the bat for more than the allowable eighteen inches and demanded a quick measurement. The home-plate umpire may have a whisk broom, but he does not customarily carry a ruler. So the bat was placed across home plate, which is seventeen inches wide. Sure enough, the pine-tar portion stretched beyond the width of the plate. The bat had heavy pine tar running nineteen to twenty inches up from the tip of the handle and lighter pine tar for another three or four inches.

What Should Have Been the Ultimate Fate of Brett's Home Run?

First, he lost the homer and the Royals lost the game. But four days later, he got the homer back. Three weeks after that, the Royals won the game.

After conferring with his fellow umps, McClelland gave the "out" sign, nullifying the home run and thereby ending the game, since Brett had represented Kansas City's final chance. The umpires reasoned that Brett had used an illegal bat, so the home run was illegal too.

Seconds later, an incredulous Brett charged at the ump. While this was going on, the Royals tried to spirit the evidence away. Pitcher Gaylord Perry—a man known to do strange things to baseballs—grabbed the bat and handed it to a teammate. It was passed around until Steve Renko, another pitcher, wound up with it. But Yankee Stadium plainclothes security men took off after the bat, and Umpire Joe Brinkman finally corralled it. "I saw guys in sport coats and ties trying to intercept the bat," Royals Manager Dick Howser remarked afterward. "It was like a Brink's robbery. Who's got the gold? Our players had it, the umpires had it. I don't know who has it—the CIA, a think tank at the Pentagon."

The Royals protested the ruling to Lee MacPhail, the American League president. During his ten years in office —a period in which some fifty protests had been sent to him—MacPhail had never overruled an umpire's decision. But this time he did. Four days after Brett hit the homer that seemingly wasn't, MacPhail restored it to him.

Declaring that "games should be won and lost on the playing field—not through technicalities of the rules," MacPhail based his decision on what he saw as the intent of the pine-tar rule. He drew a distinction between bats treated with pine tar in order to improve the grip and those altered to affect the distance a ball would travel. (An example would be a bat hollowed out and stuffed with cork.) MacPhail said the rule book cnvisioned that bats with too much pine tar should simply be prohibited. And the umpires, he said, were responsible for spotting excess pine tar. If a batter was not told to take the pine tar off or to discard a bat with excessive tar, then he was free to enjoy the fruits of his labor.

MacPhail said he had conferred with umpires, former umps and rules-committee members familiar with the creation of the pine-tar rule and had been told that it was designed simply to avoid delays in the game.

"Before the rule was put in, batters were putting pine tar all the way up their bats, and every time the ball was hit it became soiled and had to be removed from the game," MacPhail explained.

But he did not blame his umpires for calling Brett out. He conceded there had not been clear instructions on what to do in this type of situation.

MacPhail ordered that the game be resumed at Yankee Stadium with the score 5–4 in favor of the Royals. The man batting after Brett in the lineup would be coming to the plate with two out in the top of the ninth and no one on base. Since the Royals and Yanks were not scheduled to face each other again that season, MacPhail picked Thursday afternoon, August 18—when both clubs had an open date—for the game's conclusion.

But the howling was far from over. George Steinbrenner called MacPhail's decision "ridiculous" and complained that by having to resume the game, the Yankees would be forced to play thirty-one days in a row.

"Now here we are, one and a half games out of first place, and I'd like our players to have their day of relaxation," said the Yankee owner, not heretofore known for his excessive coddling of employees.

The resumption was set for a 6:00 P.M. start, but further complications were to come. The morning of August 18, three Yankee fans who had been at the original game— their ages six, seven and fourteen—went into court in the Bronx, protesting the club's decision to allow only season-ticket holders to attend the resumption for free. Everyone else was to pay $2.50 for a reserved seat or $1.00 for a bleacher seat so the Yanks could cover the $25,000 cost of opening the Stadium.

The youngsters, represented by lawyers—one of them the father of the fourteen-year-old—asked that an injunction be issued preventing the game's resumption until the merits of their cases could be heard. They claimed they had a contractual right to see the game to its conclusion without having to pay again for a seat.

In another bizarre twist to the affair, the Yankees, although a defendant in the case, joined in the request for an injunction, and Steinbrenner hired Roy Cohn of McCarthy-era notoriety to argue for him. In taking the side of the fans suing them, the Yanks maintained that their ticket policy was mandated by the league, that they couldn't provide adequate security for the resumption, and that, in any case, they wanted a full hearing on the fans' claims. Justice Oren V. Maresca issued a temporary injunction, but the American League, the other defendant, appealed. That afternoon, Justice Joseph P. Sullivan of the appellate division overturned the injunction. He noted that even if the youngsters attended the game's resumption and paid to get in, they could continue to press their case and ultimately get refunds if they prevailed.

"I guess I can express my determination best in two words—play ball," he declared.

The Yanks decided at the last moment to honor the rain checks, but that hardly inflated the gate. A grand total of 1,245 fans turned out for the resumption of the game. They saw nine minutes and forty-one seconds' worth of baseball. The final Royal batter in the top of the ninth and three Yankee hitters in the bottom of the inning were retired. It ended as a 5–4 Royal victory.

(Brett was not in uniform that day. He had belatedly been ejected from the game along with two teammates and Manager Howser for their ruckus over the umpires' ruling.)

The Yanks didn't go down without Billy Martin trying one final maneuver. When the Kansas City batter stepped to the plate, Martin put on appeal plays at first and second base. The Yanks contended that Brett had touched neither base in running out his homer. Since the original umpiring crew was not on hand, Martin figured there was no way for the Royals to prove that Brett had, in fact, touched all bases. But the new umps were prepared. Dave Phillips, the crew chief, pulled out a notarized statement by the original umpiring crew reporting that Brett and U. L. Washington, the runner on base when he hit the homer, had both touched all bags.

The pine-tar drama, begun on such a clever note by Martin, wound up with the Yankees losers on all fronts. The team dropped 13 of 22 games after MacPhail's ruling

—falling out of the pennant race—with the ballplayers attributing the collapse to their consternation over the league president's reversal. And the following December, Commissioner Bowie Kuhn fined Steinbrenner and the Yankees $250,000 for the owner's remarks blasting Mac-Phail.

As for the infamous bat, it was returned to Brett a week after the incident and wound up in a glass case at his restaurant in Hermosa Beach, California.

Two months after the 1983 season ended, a notation was added to the pine-tar rule so that umpires would have no future doubts about what to do. The umps were told that if a bat with too much pine tar somehow slips into a game, "it shall not be grounds for declaring the batter out, or ejected from the game."

As Bill Murray, the administrator of the commissioner's office, put it: "The bat goes out, but the batter doesn't. If the umpire doesn't detect it before the batter hits the ball, whatever happens happens."

Dave Magadan, the Mets' first baseman in the summer of 1991, would never be confused with one of his predecessors at the bag, fancy-fielding Keith Hernandez.

But what happened to Magadan one June night at

YOU BE THE UMPIRE!

Busch Stadium in St. Louis could not have been avoided by even the slickest of glovemen.

The Mets' ace reliever, John Franco, had come on in the bottom of the tenth inning of a 5–5 game. He had two men out with Gerald Perry on third base. The batter was Milt Thompson, a slender left-handed-hitting outfielder.

Franco delivered a fine pitch—a fastball in on the hands. Thompson swung and managed a routine grounder toward Magadan. But the pitch had broken Thompson's bat. What also came toward Magadan—heading straight for his head—was a large chunk of lumber.

Magadan instinctively sought to elude the broken bat, and it whizzed by him. But amid his preoccupation with saving his skull, the ball skipped past him too. Thompson reached first base and Perry crossed home plate.

Did Thompson's Broken Bat Illegally Interfere with Magadan's Attempt to Make a Play?

The flying piece of bat produced perfectly legal mayhem. The tainted hit stood and so did the Cardinal victory.

The rules say that when a bat breaks, play continues even if part of it sails toward a fielder.

The batter is called out for interference only if "a whole bat is thrown" toward a man trying to field the ball.

How could that happen? With a hit-and-run play on, the batter sometimes throws his bat at a wide pitch to protect the runner. If he makes contact and both bat and ball go

AT THE PLATE

flying, he'd be out despite his enterprise if the bat took aim at a would-be fielder.

Hours after the Mets-Cards game, Magadan watched the video replay in his hotel room and pronounced himself free of blame.

"There was no alternative to what I did but to take the bat on my head," he explained.

For John Franco, it was another frustration in a bewildering season. When the night was over, the left-hander had an earned run average of 0.96 but a record of 1–4. His three previous defeats had resulted from botched plays by his other infielders—Gregg Jefferies, Kevin Elster and Keith Miller.

The run he permitted against the Cardinals was only the second he had allowed all season in fifteen appearances.

"Four losses and I still don't think the ball has left the infield," he lamented. "Thank God the windows don't open in the hotel."

It began as an argument at home plate. It would conclude with FBI agents on guard near third base, protecting an umpire from a death threat.

The Boston Red Sox and Cincinnati Reds were tied, 5–5, at Riverfront Stadium in the bottom of the tenth inning of game three in the 1975 World Series. The Reds' Ed Armbrister was at bat with no one out and Cesar Geronimo on first base. Armbrister, pinch-hitting for pitcher Rawly Eastwick, bunted the ball about three feet to the right of home plate. The ball bounced high in the air, and as Carlton Fisk, the Boston catcher, grabbed it, he became entangled with Armbrister, who had paused to admire his work before heading to first.

Fisk, trying for a force-out, had to get rid of the ball while contending with Armbrister, and he needed to do it quickly because Geronimo was a speedy runner. His throw to second sailed high, caromed off the glove of shortstop Rick Burleson, and wound up in right field. Geronimo continued to third base while Armbrister made it to second. Three batters later, Joe Morgan singled home the winning run.

Should Armbrister Have Been Out for Interfering with Fisk?

Home-plate Umpire Larry Barnett, who was working his first World Series, ruled there was no interference.

"It was simply a collision," he explained afterward. "It is interference only when the batter intentionally gets in the way of the fielder."

But Rule 7.09, which seemed to cover the situation, did not mention intent. It simply said that it's interference by a batter when "he fails to avoid a fielder who is attempting to field a batted ball." Armbrister did not avoid Fisk.

It was not so simple, however. The rules are elaborated upon by written instructions given to the umpires and by the Case Book—interpretations that have the force of baseball law. In this type of play, the Case Book (the small-print material within the rule book) tells the umpire what to do. It states that "when a catcher and batter-runner going to first base have contact when the catcher is fielding the ball, there is generally no violation and nothing should be called."

The Red Sox manager, Darrell Johnson, stormed at Barnett when he made the call.

Fisk was no less enraged. After the game, he slumped in front of his locker, spitting tobacco juice on the green carpet and spewing invective. "It's a goddamn shame to lose a goddamn game because of that goddamn call," he philosophized.

The next day, Barnett, who was completing his seventh year as an American League umpire, said he and the other crew members had spent an hour and a half discussing the play after the game. Barnett said that his fellow umps agreed he had made the right call.

"I slept good last night," he said. "If I had to do it over again, I'd do it the same way."

But there were worries ahead for Barnett. The following Saturday, when the Series returned to Fenway Park for Game 6, he received a letter threatening his life and the lives of his wife and two-year-old daughter. The writer demanded that Barnett pay him $10,000 or face "a .38 caliber bullet in your head" if the Red Sox lost the Series. The letter, which mentioned "the Boston gambling world," had a name and return address, but neither checked out.

Barnett was booed when the umpires were introduced

before Game 6, and as he worked third base, agents from the FBI, which was investigating the letter, sat in the stands alongside third. They guarded him at his hotel room for the remainder of the Series.

Barnett later said he held NBC's Tony Kubek and Curt Gowdy responsible for the death threat and other mail he had received attacking him. He claimed that almost all the letters he got referred to the announcers' account of the play.

"They were very unfair to me," said Barnett. "The rule book backs me one hundred percent. They don't know the rules."

(Gowdy would say he didn't think he or Kubek did anything to incite the fans.)

The Series would be among the most memorable in baseball history. Its enduring image would be that of Carlton Fisk leaping into the air—not in anger over Barnett's ruling but in exultation over his home run off Fenway Park's left-field foul pole to win Game 6 in the twelfth inning.

But the next night, the Reds captured the World Series. Once again for the Red Sox, the anticipation of October glory ended in defeat.

 They both had the initials "Double D," but that's where the similarity ended. One was a dominating pitcher of his era, a future Hall of Famer. The other was a catcher struggling for a spot in the everyday lineup. Yet on the night of May 31, 1968, the superstar's route to a fabulous record faced a roadblock from the scrub.

Don Drysdale was seeking to become the first pitcher in National League history to record five consecutive shutouts. Going into the bottom of the ninth at Dodger Stadium, Los Angeles held a 3–0 lead over San Francisco. But Drysdale quickly got into trouble, walking Willie McCovey, yielding a single to Jim Ray Hart, and then walking Dave Marshall.

Up to the plate stepped Dick Dietz. He'd been signed for a reported $90,000 bonus in 1960, but now, in his third year with the Giants, he was hardly a star. He would, in fact, share the catching that season with the eminently forgettable Jack Hiatt and Bob Barton.

Yet it was Dietz—not Willie Mays or Willie McCovey— who had a wonderful shot at breaking up Drysdale's shutout streak. The count went to 2 balls and 2 strikes. Then Drysdale delivered a pitch headed inside. His catcher, Jeff Torborg, would later say it was a fastball while Drysdale would describe it as a slider. Either way, it came in there fast enough.

Dietz never bailed out. As he stood frozen, the ball hit him on the left arm.

YOU BE THE UMPIRE!

What Should Happen to Dietz and to Drysdale's Streak?

It seemed that a run would be forced in by the hit-batsman, ending the scoreless string. But Drysdale was in for a pleasant surprise and Dietz for a shock.

Torborg would later claim that Dietz stuck out his elbow in an effort to be hit by the pitch. Home-plate Umpire Harry Wendelstedt didn't accuse Dietz of doing that, but he did rule the pitch was simply ball three.

"The batter was in hitting position and he made absolutely no effort to move," the ump explained afterward. "He has to make some effort to get out of the way to be awarded first base."

If a batter is hit by a pitch that is outside the strike zone, he gets first base only if he attempts to avoid being touched by the baseball. If the batter does not try to elude the pitch, it's called a ball. The play is dead and no runner may advance. (If the batter is struck by a pitch within the strike zone, it's a strike whether or not the batter tries to get out of the way.)

So Drysdale once more took aim at the shutout record —if not at Dietz—as the count went to 3-and-2. Now he got Dietz to fly out to Jim Fairey in short left field. Then Ty Cline hit a smash to first that was snatched by Wes Parker, who threw home for a force-out. Finally, Jack Hiatt popped up to Parker, ending the game. Drysdale's teammates mobbed him in a World Series–like celebration.

Dodger Manager Walter Alston, who had been around baseball since the 1930s, said later it was the first time he had seen a call like that.

AT THE PLATE

"But then it is the first time I ever saw anyone get deliberately hit by a ball," he added, hardly willing to dispute the umpire's generosity.

Dietz, who had a red welt on his left arm, also had an explanation: "The pitch was hard and I just couldn't move. All I could do was flinch before it hit me."

Giant Manager Herman Franks, who had been tossed out by Wendelstedt for hotly protesting the call, hadn't cooled down afterward.

"That gutless Wendelstedt" made "the worst call I've ever seen," he fumed.

Drysdale's fifth straight shutout tied the major league mark set by Doc White of the Chicago White Sox in 1904, and now he would go for Walter Johnson's record of 56 consecutive scoreless innings, achieved in 1913.

Despite his anger, Franks did hope that Wendelstedt would be remembered long after he had passed from the scene.

"If Drysdale breaks the record now, he and Wendelstedt should share it," suggested the Giant manager. "Hell, put Wendelstedt's name on the trophy first."

Drysdale went on to get a sixth straight shutout, and he would eclipse Johnson by pitching 58 consecutive scoreless innings.

But no asterisk was placed next to Drysdale's name in the record book. Harry Wendelstedt declined a share of the glory, his final rebuff to Herman Franks.

YOU BE THE UMPIRE!

The St. Louis Browns were, as usual, providing little entertainment for their modest band of supporters as the summer of 1951 dragged on. But their boss was about to stir things up.

Holding down their accustomed spot at the bottom of the American League, the Browns were at home the afternoon of August 19 for a Sunday doubleheader with the Detroit Tigers.

Bill Veeck, the showman extraordinaire who had just bought the floundering franchise, threw a party that day. He was celebrating the fiftieth anniversary of the American League and, he claimed, the birthday of his ball club's radio sponsor, Falstaff Brewery. (Veeck later confessed that "nobody at Falstaff seemed to know exactly when their birthday was, but that was no great problem. If we couldn't prove it fell on the day we chose, neither could anyone prove that it didn't.")

Everybody entering Sportsman's Park had been treated to a can of beer, a slice of birthday cake, and a box of ice cream. The festivities, which also included a stint on the drums by Satchel Paige, drew a crowd of 18,369, the Browns' largest home turnout in four years.

In between games a seven-foot-high birthday cake was rolled onto the infield. Out popped a miniature Brownie: Eddie Gaedel, a three-foot-seven-inch, sixty-five-pound midget and sometime circus performer. He was wearing a tiny St. Louis uniform belonging to nine-year-old Bill De-

AT THE PLATE

Witt, Jr., the son of the team's vice president. On the back was a unique number: $1/8$.

The crowd had a few laughs and then the second game began. In the bottom of the first inning, Frank Saucier, a rookie outfielder, was supposed to lead off. Instead, out of the dugout came the little man who had emerged from the cake. Eddie Gaedel, carrying a toy bat, strode to the plate as a pinch hitter.

The astonished home-plate umpire, Ed Hurley, demanded credentials proving that Gaedel was really on the team.

No problem. The midget had been signed to a hundred-dollar-a-day contract and the papers had been mailed to the American League headquarters the night before. Zack Taylor, the Browns' manager, showed Hurley a copy of the contract.

Nothing in the rule book specifically barred a midget, so the umpire grudgingly allowed Gaedel to get into the batter's box.

When Veeck had told Gaedel a few days earlier how he'd be making baseball history, there was one condition: He must not mess up the stunt by trying to hit the ball.

"Eddie, I'm going to be up on the roof with a high-powered rifle watching every move you make," Veeck would remember telling Gaedel. "If you so much look as if you're going to swing, I'm going to shoot you dead."

Tiger catcher Bob Swift got down on his knees. Pitcher Bob Cain made an effort to throw strikes on his first two deliveries, but the baseball whizzed past Gaedel's chin. Finally, Cain broke down laughing and sent the next two

115

pitches about three feet over Gaedel's head. Having re-
sisted the temptation to swing, Gaedel trotted down to
first base with a walk. Outfielder Jim Delsing, after getting
a pat on the rump by his newest teammate, took Gaedel's
place on the bases.

What Is the Minimum Target for the Strike Zone?

The rule book specifies no minimum in terms of inches.
It simply deals with anatomy. Back in 1951, it read: "The
strike zone is that space over home plate which is between
the batter's armpits and the top of his knees when he as-
sumes his natural stance."

Veeck would write in his autobiography that he had
Gaedel go into a crouch when he was preparing him for
his big day and "his strike zone was just about visible to
the naked eye. I picked up a ruler and measured it for
posterity. It was 1½ inches."

So that was the target the Tiger pitcher had to find. As
for the rule book's reference to a batter's "natural stance,"
Veeck figured "since Gaedel would bat only once in his
life, whatever stance he took was, by definition, his natural
stance."

Veeck certainly had no intention of using Gaedel again.
But just to make sure, Will Harridge, the American
League president, voided his contract two days later,
vaguely citing "the best interests of baseball."

Harridge also barred Gaedel from sullying the sanctity
of the record books. The 1952 *Official Baseball Guide,*

published by *The Sporting News,* contained the records of everyone who played in at least one game during the '51 season—except for Eddie Gaedel.

But the midget could not be erased so easily. *The Baseball Encyclopedia*—"the official record of major league baseball"—gives Gaedel his due. The 1990 Macmillan edition listed him on page 992, between Len Gabrielson and Gary Gaetti.

Gaedel died in 1961 but his uniform lived on. Bill De-Witt, Jr., its original owner, kept the jersey, and in 1991 he loaned it to the Hall of Fame, where it became a prime attraction. So Bill Veeck's one-day wonder not only made it into the records books, but posthumously received recognition by baseball's shrine.

Eddie Gaedel's wonderful moment in the sun would be remembered many years later by Frank Saucier, the only man in major league history to be pinch-hit for by a midget. Saucier recalled how the man with the inch-and-a-half strike zone was transformed, in his own eyes, into a giant of the game.

"When he went down to first base, he stopped two or three times and took his hat off and bowed to the crowd. When he came back to the dugout, I said, 'Eddie, you really kind of clowned that up a bit, didn't you?' "

"And he said, 'Man, I felt like Babe Ruth.' "

YOU BE THE UMPIRE!

Mickey Owen caught for thirteen seasons in the major leagues, but he's remembered for a single moment: the dropped third strike in the 1941 World Series that made him a "goat" for the ages.

Jimmy Wilson, also a catcher, was the central figure in another Series incident involving an apparent strike three. That play has long been forgotten, but it was a lot stranger than Owen's muff on Tommy Henrich's infamous strikeout.

The Philadelphia Athletics were facing the St. Louis Cardinals at Sportsman's Park in Game 2 of the 1931 Series. These were truly the dominant teams of the day. The A's had beaten the Cards in the 1930 Series. Now, boasting a lineup including Mickey Cochrane, Jimmie Foxx, Al Simmons and Jimmy Dykes, they were battling a Cardinal team led by Pepper Martin, Sunny Jim Bottomley, Frankie Frisch and Chick Hafey.

After losing the opener of the '31 Series, the Cardinals took a 2–0 lead into the ninth inning of the second game thanks to the daring baserunning of Pepper Martin, who had scored both runs. But Wild Bill Hallahan, a 19-game winner that season, suddenly began living up to his nickname by issuing walks to Foxx and Dykes. The left-hander was faced with runners on first and second and two out. Jimmy Moore, a reserve outfielder, came up to pinch-hit for A's pitcher George Earnshaw. The count went to one ball and two strikes and then Moore foul-tipped a pitch.

AT THE PLATE

Had Wilson caught the ball, it would have all been over. But it squirted out of his mitt.

The next delivery was a low curve. As Hallahan pitched, the runners took off. Moore swung and missed. The ball went into the dirt but Wilson stayed with the pitch and scooped it up. Seeing Foxx headed for third, he fired the ball there, but Foxx slid in ahead of the grab by Jake Flowers.

Could Moore Have Tried for First Base Despite His Missed Swing on Strike Three, and If So, Why Would Wilson Throw to Third?

Wilson had kept a tough pitch from going wild in contrast to Mickey Owen, who ten years later would let Hugh Casey's sweeping curve (Casey would later claim it was a spitter) get past him to the backstop. But the A's-Cards game was not over.

For a third strike to be legally caught, the ball must be in the catcher's mitt before it hits the ground. Scooping the baseball up is a lot more impressive than letting it get through, but it's still not a catch.

The rule book says that a batter stays alive if a third strike is not caught by the catcher unless there's a man on first base and less than two out.

Since there were two men down, Moore could try to get to first base. (It was still scored as a strikeout for the pitcher.)

All the Cardinal catcher had to do to retire Moore was

throw to first. Since Wilson had the ball, this was no overwhelming task. But when he saw Foxx head to third, Wilson became disoriented and committed a mental error by throwing there.

"I was playing the double steal," he would explain. "The base runners took a flying start. I saw that Hallahan's pitch was very low, that it was going to hit the ground before it reached me. I set myself to make a pickup of the ball and a fast throw to third. It didn't enter my head that Moore would swing at so bad a pitch. I guess I didn't realize he actually swung until after the ball left my hand on its way to third.

"A moment later I realized that all I would have had to do was throw as slowly as I wanted to first base."

Moore had dallied at the plate, figuring he'd failed on the Athletics' last chance, but Eddie Collins, the third-base coach, yelled at him to get moving. So he ran to first and got there by the time the dust had cleared at third with Foxx safe.

Hundreds of Cardinal fans had poured onto the field, but the celebration was cut short and they were shooed back to the stands.

Now the Athletics had the bases loaded with Max Bishop, their leadoff man and second baseman, coming to the plate. Bishop lifted a pop-up heading toward the seats down the right-field line. Sunny Jim Bottomley, the Cards' first baseman, ran back, drifted toward the railing, dived across a bull-pen bench crowded with Philadelphia pitchers, and leaned into the field boxes to make a sensational catch.

AT THE PLATE

Wild Bill Hallahan had his shutout. Jimmy Wilson—though charged with an error for his gaffe—had been rescued from World Series infamy.

Bob Borkowski stuck around for six years in the big leagues, but the outfielder seldom made it into a starting lineup. In the early 1950s, Borkowski was with the Cincinnati Reds, but he was eclipsed by an array of power hitters—Ted Kluszewski, Gus Bell and Wally Post. One night in September 1954, however, Borkowski was the center of attention with Bell and Post playing supporting roles in a mix-up bringing much grief to the umpires.

Borkowski pinch-hit against Warren Spahn in the ninth inning at Milwaukee's County Stadium with Post on first base and Bell at second. There was one out and the Reds were trailing the Braves by 3–1.

Not surprisingly, Borkowski struck out. But when he saw the ball get past catcher Del Crandall, he took off for first base. Post stayed put, but Bell broke for third. Crandall caught up with the baseball, then fired it to third baseman Eddie Mathews. The throw arrived too late to nail Bell, but Mathews saw that Borkowski still hadn't reached first. He threw over there, but the toss hit Borkowski in the back and bounced into right field. Now both Bell and Post got going and crossed the plate, apparently tying the game.

YOU BE THE UMPIRE!

Was Borkowski Entitled to First Base and Did the Runs Scored by Bell and Post Count?

Borkowski either didn't know about or had forgotten the strikeout rule for that situation: If there is a man on first and less than two down, a batter who strikes out on a wild pitch or passed ball is not permitted to try for first base.

The rule is designed to prevent a catcher from intentionally dropping a third strike, then starting a double play.

Since the Reds had men on first and second and only one out, Borkowski had only one option—returning to the bench.

But Bell had every right to try for third base when the pitch went astray and Crandall did the correct thing by throwing down there. Now, however, Borkowski's futile attempt to reach first complicated things. Mathews should never have tried to throw him out after failing to get Bell at third—Borkowski was already erased by the rule book.

Since Borkowski was, in effect, a phantom runner, should the Braves have suffered when their throw ricocheted off him, bringing his two teammates across the plate? On the other hand, should the Reds have suffered because Mathews made a throw he didn't need to make?

The four umpires huddled for eighteen minutes, then came up with a ruling. There was no question that Borkowski had made the second out when he fanned. But home-plate Umpire Hal Dixon called Bell out as well—he was penalized because Borkowski had been found guilty of interference by drawing a throw via his illegal scamper toward first. The Braves' Crandall was given credit for an unassisted double play, being awarded putouts on Borkowski's strikeout and on Bell. End of inning, end of game.

The Reds' manager, Birdie Tebbetts, had argued that since Milwaukee's Mathews showed no higher a baseball IQ than Cincinnati's Borkowski, the throw to first base should not have counted. He proposed a compromise: Have both Bell and Post returned to the bases and resume the game with two out.

Tebbetts asked the umpires to apply a basic principle: What would the situation be if the illegal play had not occurred?

But the umps stuck to their ruling, so Tebbetts protested to Warren Giles, the National League president. Although Giles declined to fault the umpires for their decision under game pressure, he upheld the protest the following day.

The way Giles saw it, this was not a brazen case of interference just because Borkowski ran to first when he was already a goner.

"Elements of interference and confusion both existed, but not to an extent sufficient to declare Bell out," he said.

He also noted that the outcome of the game could affect how the Braves, Reds and three other teams would finish in the standings. (The Giants had clinched the pennant but the players on first-division teams would be divvying up some of the World Series receipts.)

Giles ordered that the game be resumed with the following situation: two men out, Bell on third and Post on second.

The Reds had moved on to Chicago for a weekend series ending the season, but Giles ordered them back to Milwaukee. On Friday afternoon, September 24—two days after the game with the mutual gaffes—the clubs returned to the field. Now the Reds made the most of their second chance. Johnny Temple singled on the first pitch from Dave Jolly, who had been brought in to relieve Spahn, sending home Bell and pinch-runner Nino Escalara to tie the score. But in the bottom of the ninth, the Braves' George (Catfish) Metkovich drove home the winning run with a single of his own.

In another strange twist, the Braves faced two different teams that day. After the game with the Reds was completed, they played their regularly scheduled opponent, the Cardinals. The Reds' players had dressed for the game's resumption at a downtown hotel while the Cardinals used the visitors' clubhouse. All three teams took batting practice and then the Reds and Cards shared one dugout.

A notation was later added to the rule book saying that if a player continues to run "after he has been put out, he shall not by that act alone be considered as confusing, hindering or impeding the fielders."

So if a play like this one came up today, the runners might be allowed to score. The key question would be whether the batter had deliberately run to first in the hopes of drawing a throw. If the umpire had evidence of that—if he yelled "you're out" to a latter-day Bob Borkowski but he kept going—then any wild throw would be nullified and a latter-day Gus Bell at third would be out if he tried to score. But if the batter who'd been struck out ran simply because he was unaware of the rules, there would be no interference. The team in the field would suffer the consequences of trying to cut down a runner who had already been erased.

Not long after his gaffe, Borkowski was gone from the Reds. He finished up the 1955 season—and his big league career as well—with, of all clubs, the World Series champion Brooklyn Dodgers. But with the likes of Duke Snider and Carl Furillo in the outfield, there was even less chance for him to see action—and foul up an entire umpiring team—than there had been with the Reds. Borkowski came to the plate a grand total of 19 times for the Dodgers. On 6 of those at-bats he repeated the deed he'd be best known for—he struck out.

When a manager utters the "magic word" in arguing with an umpire or makes physical contact with him, he's guaranteed to spend the rest of the day cooling off in the clubhouse. But even when histrionics are minimal, there are circumstances bringing an automatic ejection. A manager—or any player or coach leaving his position to approach the plate—is supposed to be thrown out the moment he argues whether a pitch was a ball or strike.

But a manager or catcher can dispute an umpire's call on a checked swing. The appeal can be made only when the home-plate ump calls a ball. If asked to get another opinion the umpire is required to defer to his fellow ump at first or third base. That umpire, presumably having a better view, may decide that the batter went around and then will signal a strike.

When the Minneapolis Millers visited the Omaha Cardinals in Game 3 of a play-off to determine the 1955 American Association champions, the home-plate and third-base umpires were not exactly working in harmony.

It was the seventh inning of a scoreless game. Omaha's Stu Miller, working on a no-hitter, had an 0-and-1 count on leadoff batter Monte Irvin, the former Giant then near the end of his career. Irvin took a half swing on the next delivery. Home-plate Umpire Eddie Taylor called the pitch a ball, but third-base Umpire Bob Stewart, without waiting for an appeal, ruled that Irvin had broken his wrists and called it a strike. Taylor refused to be overruled and insisted the count was 1-and-1. Now Miller came to the plate to ask Taylor why he wouldn't accept Stewart's ruling.

What Should Be the Correct Count and What Should Happen to Miller?

Taylor, no doubt angry over the other umpire's rush to judgment, stuck to his call—keeping the count at 1-and-1—and then kicked Miller out of the game. Taylor considered Miller's argument at that point to be a dispute over a simple ball or strike call, thereby bringing an automatic ejection.

That brought the Omaha fans into the act. Furious that

AT THE PLATE

their pitcher was thrown out while working on a no-hitter, they began tossing seat cushions onto the field. Now Bill Bergesch, the Omaha general manager, asked the umps to consult with the league president, Ed Doherty, who was in the stands.

Doherty quickly overruled the home-plate ump's ejection of Miller although allowing the count to be 1-and-1 instead of 0-and-2 as pronounced prematurely by the third-base ump.

Then it was Minneapolis's turn to howl. Bill Rigney, the Millers' manager, announced he would protest the game if his team lost, contending that Miller, once thrown out, couldn't be thrown back in.

Miller returned to the mound and retired Irvin and the next batter, but then gave up a home run to Bill Lennon, who had slugged 64 homers the season before in the Southern Association. The no-hitter and shutout were gone. But Omaha got three runs in the eighth inning and won the game, 3–1.

So Minneapolis went ahead with its protest, prompting a midnight meeting at a downtown hotel involving league president Doherty, both managers and the four umpires.

When the summit ended, Doherty upheld the protest. Reversing his own ruling of the night before, he now agreed that Miller had been rightfully ejected. The game was ordered to be replayed the following afternoon from the point where Miller had a 1-and-1 count on Irvin.

When play resumed, with the no-hitter again intact, Bob Tiefenauer went to the mound to replace Miller. He got Irvin to hit a grounder, but shortstop Dick Schofield booted the ball. The next batter sacrificed, and then Lennon—the man who had hit the homer the night before—arrived at the plate again. This time he walloped a triple, presumably becoming the first batter ever to break up a no-hitter twice in the same game.

Minneapolis went on to beat Omaha, 7–2. Later that day, the Millers captured the regularly scheduled game to sweep the series and go on to the Junior World Series against the International League champions.

So the game Omaha thought it had won turned out to be lost, thanks to a third-base umpire who had butted in, bringing on a blowup that ultimately saw a pitcher with a no-hitter get booted out.

4

AROUND THE BASES

It was a gaffe more worthy of the Black Sox than the White Sox.

The scene was Comiskey Park, the second game of the 1917 World Series. Urban (Red) Faber, the spitballing starting pitcher for the Chicago White Sox that afternoon, was the runner at second base. Buck Weaver was at third. The batter was Chicago's leadoff man, Nemo Leibold.

As the New York Giant pitcher Ferdie Schupp delivered the ball to the plate, there was a flurry of activity on the base paths. But Weaver wasn't trying to steal home. He was ensconced at third base when, to his horror, he saw Faber sprinting toward him. The pitcher had decided to steal third, totally forgetting there was a runner already there.

Catcher Bill Rariden whipped the ball down to third base-

man Heinie Zimmerman, who made the tag on Faber, clearing the congestion at the bag and ending the inning.

Two Octobers later, the White Sox would throw a World Series to the Cincinnati Reds, and that ball club would forever be known as the infamous "Black Sox." But even at their most brazen, those fixers wouldn't dream of pulling a stunt like Red Faber's jaunt.

Running the bases can be quite an adventure. The Faber-Weaver combo would, in fact, be outdone by the Brooklyn Dodgers a decade later. The "Daffiness Boys" once put three men on the same bag.

Sometimes there's a contrary kind of mess: A runner neglects to touch a base en route to the next station.

And, in the haste to circle the bases, more than one ballplayer has passed the runner in front of him.

For every snafu there's a rule to set things straight—and get tempers flaring as well.

But so much for malfeasance on the base paths. What about brilliant displays of baserunning?

How about that 1950 affair down in Carolina when Bill Kearns of the Asheville Tourists led the opposing team's catcher on a merry chase?

Asheville had the bases loaded in a Southern League game against Knoxville when a grounder was hit to shortstop. Kearns, the runner at third, slid into home just as the throw from short pulled catcher Jack Aragon off the plate.

Aragon thought that Kearns had missed home. The catcher could have simply touched the plate for a force-out, but he took off after Kearns instead. He chased him into the dugout, *then pursued him up the runway and into the clubhouse. Finally, he made the tag.*

Kearns had actually touched the plate, so he was safe to begin with. And while he was leading Aragon on that little romp, the other three runners dashed around the bases.

Four men scored—on a ground ball to shortstop.

The Miracle Mets of 1969 rode to their incredible World Series championship on the arms of Tom Seaver and Jerry Koosman. But three players in understudy roles—Rod Gaspar, Al Weis and J. C. Martin—figured in a memorable October moment.

Holding a lead of two games to one over the Baltimore Orioles, the Mets went to the tenth inning of Game 4 at Shea Stadium tied, 1–1.

Jerry Grote, their catcher, led off with a fly to short left field that Don Buford lost in the sun. It dropped for a double. Now, enter the scrubs. Gaspar, a reserve outfielder, ran for Grote. The Oriole pitcher, Dick Hall, intentionally walked Weis, a backup infielder during the regular season who had reached base seven times in the first three games and had won Game 2 with a ninth-inning single. Mets Manager Gil Hodges then ordered the left-handed-batting Martin, a substitute catcher–first baseman, to hit for Seaver. Lefty Pete Richert replaced the right-handed Hall.

YOU BE THE UMPIRE!

Martin put down a beautiful bunt on Richert's first pitch, the ball dying ten feet toward first base. Richert picked the baseball up and fired toward Davey Johnson, the second baseman, who was covering first. Boog Powell, the first baseman, had charged in, anticipating the sacrifice.

Martin was running to the left of—or just inside—the foul line. Richert's throw struck him on the left wrist a couple of strides before he reached first base, and the ball caromed into right field. Gaspar raced to home plate.

What Should Happen to Martin?

The umpires should have called Martin out—but they didn't. The Orioles should have screamed—but they stayed silent.

When there's a possibility of a throw to first base from behind the batter, he is supposed to run within the "three-foot lane" that was created to avoid the kind of disaster that befell the Orioles.

A white line, three feet to the right of the foul line and parallel to it, runs for the last forty-five feet of the distance between home plate and first base. A batter must be called out if he runs either outside (to the right of) the lane or inside (to the left of) the lane and "in the umpire's judgment interferes with the fielder making the throw to first base."

These were the days before "instant replay," but photographs clearly showed that Martin was running with both feet inside the foul line when the ball struck him. There was no question that his leftward leanings had caused the throw to go wild because the ball had hit him on the left wrist.

But neither Shag Crawford, the home-plate umpire, nor Lou DiMuro, the first-base ump, made the out call. And so the Mets had a tainted victory. The next day, when a furor erupted, there was no explanation from the umpires. They refused to talk.

Davey Johnson said afterward that he was sure Martin had been running within the three-foot lane. "He was close, but he was in that box," said Johnson.

Where was Oriole Manager Earl Weaver while his ball club was being robbed? That dirt-kicker extraordinaire had been banished back in the third inning by Crawford for arguing a strike call on Mark Belanger.

(Although disputing ball-and-strike calls is supposed to bring an automatic ejection, it's not easy for a manager to get thrown out of a World Series game. Weaver was the first one to earn that distinction since the Cubs' Charlie Grimm had been ejected from a Chicago-Detroit game in the 1935 Series.)

Billy Hunter, a coach who took over upon Weaver's departure, saw eye-to-eye with Davey Johnson. "From the bench I was sure he was in foul territory," Hunter said, meaning he thought that Martin was running within the designated lane.

That play was the second one in two innings where the Mets seemed blessed. In the bottom of the ninth, Ron Swoboda had kept the Orioles from taking the lead by making a fantastic diving catch of a liner to right field by Brooks Robinson.

The next afternoon, Jerry Koosman pitched the Mets to the World Series championship.

Fifteen years later, Davey Johnson would once again be seeing things the Mets' way. By then, of course, he was forced to: He had become their manager.

It was the great October mismatch as the Atlanta Braves faced the Minnesota Twins in Game 2 of the 1991 World Series.

The ball clubs themselves were evenly matched. They had both leapt from last-place finishes the previous season and would battle into the seventh game in one of the most exciting Series ever played. The mismatch was between two ballplayers: the Braves' Ron Gant, six feet and 172 pounds, and the Twins' Kent Hrbek, six feet four inches and 253 pounds.

The Braves were trailing, 2–1, in the third inning at the Metrodome with two men out. Gant came to the plate and lined a single to left field off Kevin Tapani, sending Lonnie Smith from first base to third. Left fielder Dan Gladden, trying to throw Smith out, fired the ball wide of third, between the foul line and pitcher's mound. Tapani picked up the baseball and then saw that Gant had made a wide turn around first. The pitcher threw the ball to Hrbek, the first baseman.

Gant got back to the bag, but then he became entangled with Hrbek, who tagged him. Suddenly, Gant was off the base. Umpire Drew Coble called him out, ending the inning and beginning a huge argument.

Did Gant Have an Absolute Right to the Bag Once He Touched It?

Once Gant had possession of the bag, might didn't make right. The massive Hrbek could not legally push him off the base, then apply the tag.

So Umpire Coble had to decide—without benefit of a TV replay—whether Gant had been muscled off the base by Hrbek.

The ump ruled that after Gant had retouched first, he lost control of his body and was in the air when he was tagged.

"His momentum was carrying toward the first-base dugout," Coble told reporters after the game. "When he did that, he began to switch feet. He tried to pick up one foot and bring the other one down. That just carried him more to the first-base dugout. Hrbek took the throw low and tried to tag him as his feet were coming up. As he did that, he [Gant] just went over the top of him."

Gant saw it this way:

"He pushed me. Everyone on TV and in the stadium knew I was on the base. If he hadn't pulled me off, I would

135

YOU BE THE UMPIRE!

have stayed on the base. I didn't know you could push a guy off the base."

Hrbek—a big fan of professional wrestling with a physique to match—had a bizarre explanation, considering the disparity in size between the two men.

"He fell on top of me. He pushed me over."

When Coble made the out call, Braves Manager Bobby Cox came hurtling out of his dugout as if he were the one who'd been given a mighty shove.

But no amount of arguing by Cox or by Gant—who had to be restrained by first-base coach Pat Corrales and the manager—could change Coble's mind.

Instead of Dave Justice coming to the plate with two out and two on, the inning was over. And the Braves went on to lose the game, 3–2.

The TV replay seemed to show that Gant's right foot was on the base when Hrbek tagged him and that Hrbek had lifted Gant's leg off the bag with his glove hand.

But the Braves displayed grudging admiration for Hrbek when the heat of battle had settled.

"Hrbek is a hard player who will do anything to win," remarked Corrales. "I told him later I didn't blame him. He got away with it."

"If you can get the edge and help him off the bag, so be it," said Terry Pendleton, the Braves' third baseman. "You're trying to win."

Sid Bream, the Atlanta first baseman, remembered how he had once gotten away with the same maneuver, victimizing the Mets' Vince Coleman.

AROUND THE BASES

The victim of the moment—Ron Gant—proved less than charitable.

He wasn't about to assault the umpire and he couldn't very well tear into the hulking Hrbek.

So Gant took his anger out on a source unable to fight back: Upon returning to the dugout, he destroyed a couple of Gatorade coolers.

The summer of 1908 brought a National League pennant race unprecedented for excitement. Three teams battled down to the final weekend —and even then matters were not decided. It would take a play-off of a tie game in order to produce a champion.

That season also produced the ultimate baseball "goat."

Act I

On the afternoon of Friday, September 4, the Pirates and Cubs were in a scoreless tie in the bottom of the tenth inning at Pittsburgh's Exposition Park. On the mound for Chicago was Mordecai (Three-Finger) Brown, renowned for his ability to make a baseball dance as it tumbled from a pitching hand mangled in a childhood accident. Pittsburgh had loaded the bases with two out, and a rookie outfielder named John (Chief) Wilson was at the plate.

YOU BE THE UMPIRE!

Wilson smacked the ball into center field, sending player-manager Fred Clarke home from third base for an apparent 1–0 victory.

Now complications arose. Johnny Evers, the Cub second baseman, a shrimp of a ballplayer at 115 pounds but a student of the rule book, noticed that the play wasn't quite complete. Pittsburgh's Warren Gill, the runner at first, had stopped halfway to second base and then returned to the dugout as soon as Wilson's drive landed safely. Evers yelled for Jimmy Slagle, the center fielder, to throw the ball to him, and he stepped on second base. He then accosted Hank O'Day, the lone umpire, and demanded that he declare a force play. Since no run can score on an inning-ending force, the game was still 0–0, according to Evers.

Should Clarke's Run Have Counted?

According to the rule book, this was indeed a force-out. But O'Day had headed for his locker room as soon as Wilson's drive dropped safely. He maintained he hadn't seen Evers step on second. At any rate, except for the man coming home, runners customarily didn't advance to the next base in this type of game-ending situation, and O'Day wasn't about to set a precedent. So he refused to call a force-out.

The Cubs appealed to Harry Pulliam, the National League president, but he declined to intervene. "I think the baseball public prefers to see games settled on the field and not in this office," he said.

So Clarke's run stood, and the Pirates kept their 1–0 victory.

Act II

As the 1908 season moved toward its climax, the Cubs, Pirates and Giants were fighting for the pennant. On Tuesday, September 23, the Cubs played the Giants at the Polo Grounds. They went to the last of the ninth inning with the score tied, 1–1.

The Giants rallied and they got two men on base with two down. A nineteen-year-old rookie named Fred Merkle was the runner on first, Moose McCormick the runner at third. The batter, Al Bridwell, hit a drive that landed in right-center field to send McCormick home with what appeared to be the winning run. Merkle took a few steps toward second base, but then came a change of direction that would change his fortunes until the day he died. He ran to the outfield clubhouse as delirious fans swarmed onto the grass to celebrate.

It was the same turn of events as in the Cubs-Pirates game nineteen days before, only this time it was Fred Merkle and not Warren Gill who strayed. Once again, the Chicago second baseman was Johnny Evers and the umpire was Hank O'Day. Once again, Evers called for the ball from the outfield and then chased after O'Day, maintaining he had created a force play by touching second base and therefore had nullified the apparent winning run.

Since Warren Gill Did Not Have to Live Up to the Letter of Baseball Law, What Should the Ruling Have Been on Fred Merkle?

O'Day evidently had done some thinking about his earlier decision—or nondecision. This time he ruled that Evers had indeed made a force play. The game was therefore still knotted at 1–1.

(Amid the tumult, however, it was never determined whether the baseball Evers grasped as he touched second was the same one that Bridwell had hit.)

By now, Giant fans were all over the field, thrilled with their heroes and unaware of the ump's ruling. O'Day presumably envisioned paying with his life if he ordered the teams back from their clubhouses. So he conveniently decided it was too dark to continue and sent everyone home. The game went into the books as a tie.

It would be the most controversial episode in baseball history until the great pine-tar dispute.

The enraged Giants appealed all the way to the National League's directors, but they upheld the umpire, calling Merkle's failure to go to second base "a reckless, inexcusable blunder." The league then announced that the game would be replayed in its entirety if the outcome would have a bearing on the pennant race.

Two weeks later, the regular schedule ended with the

AROUND THE BASES

Cubs and Giants tied for first place, each having played 153 games to a decision. The Pirates were one-half game back. On Thursday, October 8, the Cubs and Giants played the tie off on an afternoon of enormous frenzy. Some 30,000 fans jammed the Polo Grounds and tens of thousands more strained for a glimpse from elevated railroad tracks, from apartment-building roofs, from the limbs of trees. The Cubs won the game, 4–2, and captured the pennant with the second chance provided by "Merkle's boner."

Though Fred Merkle had merely followed baserunning custom, he would become the most vilified figure in baseball history. He was an intelligent player and went on to a fine career that spanned sixteen seasons, yet he'd always be taunted as a "bonehead" and the expression would enter the American vernacular.

A decade after Merkle's death in 1956, Al Bridwell, the man whose drive to the outfield set the bizarre events in motion, looked back on that afternoon.

"I wish I'd never gotten that hit," he lamented. "I wish I'd struck out instead. If I'd have done that, then it would have spared Fred a lot of unfair humiliation.

"Anyway, he's gone now. The newspapers crucified him. The fans ragged him unmercifully the rest of his life. But now his worries are over. Only thing I lost out of it was a base hit. Didn't get credit for that base hit. They decided it was a force-out at second instead of a single. Well, what can you do? Those things happen."

YOU BE THE UMPIRE!

Act III

Eight decades later, Dave Kingman seemed to follow in the footsteps of Warren Gill and Fred Merkle.

When the Yankees' Dave Righetti threw ball four to the Athletics' Steve Henderson with two out and the bases loaded in the bottom of the ninth inning, the game at the Oakland Coliseum one Saturday afternoon in May 1985 was seemingly over. Carney Lansford trotted home for the winning run in an 8–7 Oakland victory.

But Yankee Manager Billy Martin wasn't ready to give up.

Dave Kingman, the runner on first base, had declined to exert himself by going all the way down to the second-base bag. He headed toward his dugout as soon as Henderson drew his walk.

As Kingman strolled in the general vicinity of the pitcher's mound, his teammates and coaches yelled for him to reverse course and get on down to second. Clete Boyer, the third-base coach, was screaming the loudest. "I was about to tackle him," he said later.

Kingman got the message and sped toward second. Ron Hassey, the Yankee catcher, fired the ball there, but Kingman slid under shortstop Dale Berra's tag and was called safe by Umpire Rick Reed.

Storming onto the field, Martin demanded that Kingman be called out for leaving the base paths and that the run be nullified.

"Kingman ran out of the base line before the runner touched home plate," Martin argued.

AROUND THE BASES

Should Kingman's Wayward Route Have Nullified Lansford's Run?

Although Warren Gill's failure to go to second base should have erased that Pirate run back in 1908 and Fred Merkle's failure to reach second did, in fact, negate the big Giant run a few weeks later, Kingman had done nothing illegal.

The situation here was not the same as in the Gill and Merkle incidents.

Because a bases-loaded walk was involved, Kingman couldn't be forced out at second base. And he could not be called out for straying from the base path.

"The only time a guy can be called out for running out of the baseline is if he's trying to avoid a tag," said Umpire Rich Garcia.

Kingman did not, in fact, have to reach second base at all. His coach's histrionics and the slide at second were so much theatrics.

The rule book says that when the winning run is scored "as the result of a base on balls . . . the umpire shall not declare the game ended until the runner forced to advance from third has touched home base and the batter-runner has touched first base."

Nothing is said about the runner on first having to touch second or the runner on second having to reach third.

What was going on in Kingman's mind when he decided to foresake second base? Had he known the rule, then made his mad dash only because his coach and teammates confused him? Nah.

"I just short-circuited," he confessed.

YOU BE THE UMPIRE!

The big leaguers of the early 1900s came to the diamond from factories, farms and mines. Their prime intellectual pursuit was a scanning of the sports pages. But Fred Tenney stood a man apart. He was an alumnus of Brown University, the first college graduate to be a major league star. And in an era when most ball-players were roughnecks, his only vice was said to be the use of chewing tobacco.

He'd been a slick-fielding first baseman and an outstanding hitter for fourteen seasons with Boston's National League club before being traded to the Giants in 1908. That season, on the afternoon of Friday, July 31, Tenney displayed an uncommon imagination.

He was the runner at first base and Luther (Dummy) Taylor was on third. It was the eighth inning of a game against the Cardinals at the Polo Grounds, and the Giants were romping, 9–2.

As pitcher Bugs Raymond held the ball, Tenney broke for second base and he stole it. Raymond threw to third, hoping to catch Taylor napping, but he got back to the bag safely. The baserunning adventures were not, however, quite over. Seconds later, Tenney ran backward, "stealing" first base. When Raymond threw his next pitch, Tenney took off once again and "stole" second base for the second time.

AROUND THE BASES

Could Tenney Legally Steal a Base Going Backward?

The next day's newspapers reported that Tenney had been toying with the Cardinals since the game seemed out of reach for them. The headline in *The New York Times* groused: BURLESQUE ON GREAT NATIONAL GAME. *The New York Evening Journal* credited "Fred, the funny Puritan" with "a new joke."

But there might have been a method to the apparent madness. Tenney may have been trying to draw throws to second in the hope that Taylor would then be able to run home. When the maneuver didn't work the first time, he had to "steal" first in order to get a second chance at a double steal. With New York way ahead, he didn't have much to lose.

The modern-day rule book makes it clear that a runner can't steal a base backward in the hope that he may eventually help another runner go forward.

If a player "runs the bases in reverse order for the purpose of confusing the defense," the umpire is supposed to call him out.

But back in 1908, the team in the field had to give the umpire an official wake-up call. When Tenney returned to first base, the Cardinals were required to tag him there or throw the ball to second base in order for him to be erased. They did neither. And, as Sam Crane, a ballplayer turned sportswriter, explained in the *Evening Journal:* "It was not in Umpire Johnstone's province to put the Cardinals wise."

The official scorer was unimpressed by Tenney's motion

studies. He gave him only one stolen base, for the first time he had gone down to second.

Amid all this, Taylor never came home from third base. But the Giants closed it out as 9–2 winners.

These were the days when readers of the sports pages expected cheering from the press box. W. W. Aulick, the *Times*'s man on the scene, was happy to oblige.

"When it gets so that we steal second and then race back to first and then try to steal second again, and then win by a ridiculously large margin, it makes us feel as if we could play armless pitchers and legless base runners and still top the tally," he crowed.

When they faced each other at Ebbets Field on June 3, 1918, the Cardinals and Dodgers were both at the bottom of the National League.

But on that afternoon, the batters for both clubs performed like world-beaters. After five innings, Brooklyn held an 11–9 lead.

In the sixth, the Cardinals' Doug Baird was on second base when the batter, Walton Cruise, lifted a shallow fly. Convinced that the Dodger left fielder, Zach Wheat, couldn't reach the ball, Baird sped to the third-base bag. Then he looked back and saw that Wheat—a future Hall of Famer—was closing in on the baseball. Suddenly having second thoughts (or more precisely, thoughts of second base), Baird began to run back toward the bag from whence he had come. When he got about twenty feet toward second, he realized that his first instinct had been the correct one—the ball bounced in front of the lunging Wheat.

Now Baird, having dallied, decided to take the most direct route to home plate. He went there diagonally—cutting across the diamond instead of touching third base again—and scored the Cards' tenth run.

Should Baird's Run Have Counted?

Umpire Cy Rigler ruled that the run was legitimate. But that's not how Wilbert Robinson, the Dodger manager, saw it. Robbie had been around for quite a while—he was the catcher on the roughneck Baltimore Oriole teams of the 1890s. Those clubs were famous for breaking the rules with an assortment of tricks. Third baseman John McGraw would delay base runners rounding his bag by grabbing their belts while the umpire's attention was elsewhere. But even a runner frantically seeking to avoid a confrontation with McGraw would be loath to try a shortcut like the one Baird had pulled off against Brooklyn. So Robinson stormed out to dispute matters with Rigler. He lost the argument. And the Dodgers went on to lose the game. Coming up with three runs in the twelfth inning, the Cardinals emerged with a 15–12 victory.

The Dodgers protested Rigler's ruling, and almost two weeks later, John Tener, the National League president, overruled his umpire and ordered that the game be stricken from the record books and replayed.

Once a runner reaches a base and retreats, he must touch that bag again before going beyond it. Or, as Tener put it, "the way to home plate is by third base."

So all 27 runs and 36 hits (23 by the Cardinals) produced that day were simply for exercise. It was a particularly galling afternoon for Ollie O'Mara, the Dodgers' starting third baseman. After getting a base hit in his first at-bat, he had been knocked from the game in the second inning when he was conked on the nose by Cardinal pitcher Lee Meadows's vicious grounder. The National League president, by wiping out all the records that day, had erased O'Mara's base hit. But John Tener could hardly undo the sore nose.

The scene shifts to Baltimore. It's not the old Orioles of Wilbert Robinson and John McGraw who are in the field, but the modern-day Birds.

It was July 25, 1982, and the Orioles were facing the Athletics at Memorial Stadium. With one out in the fifth inning and Baltimore leading by 3–0, an Oakland batter singled. The next hitter, Dwayne Murphy, sliced a high fly into the left-field corner on a hit-and-run play. The ball landed safely and then bounced into the seats for a ground-rule double.

AROUND THE BASES

The runner on first, who was off with the pitch, dived into second base. But then, figuring the ball might be caught, he retreated slightly toward first base. Finally, seeing the baseball drop in, he ran to third. But he didn't touch second base a second time.

What Happened to the Runner?

The Orioles put on an appeal play, pitcher Dennis Martinez tossing the ball to second baseman Rich Dauer, who stepped on the bag. Umpire Nick Bremigan then called the runner out for failing to retouch second.

Billy Martin—that season wearing an Athletics hat in his tour of American League dugouts—argued that the runner could go to third via any route he chose since the ball hit by Murphy was dead when it bounded into the seats. But Bremigan insisted that the ground-rule double did not free the runner from his customary path. Even when a base runner is entitled to advance, he must touch the bases he passes.

The situation was similar to the one involving the Cardinals' Doug Baird back in 1918, although the ball wasn't dead in that adventure. Baird may be forgiven his blunder since he was not exactly one of baseball's legendary base runners. But the Athletic who ran himself out of a play should have known better. It was none other than the game's greatest base-stealer, Rickey Henderson.

YOU BE THE UMPIRE!

Some of the stories about Babe Herman are patently untrue. He was never hit on the head by a fly ball. ("On the shoulders don't count," he once said.) He never left his son stranded at Ebbets Field after a game. ("I remembered him as soon as I had gone about two and a half blocks.") But he did once take a lighted cigar out of his pocket and he most certainly was the central figure in the three-men-on-a-base episode that symbolized the "Daffiness Boys" Brooklyn Dodgers of the 1920s.

The Dodgers were tied, 1–1, with the Boston Braves in a game at Ebbets Field on August 15, 1926. It was the seventh inning, and Brooklyn had loaded the bases with one out. George Mogridge, an aging left-hander, was the pitcher. At the plate was a left-handed-batting twenty-three-year-old rookie with blond hair, buck teeth and slumping shoulders. Babe Herman swung and drove the ball up against the right-field wall.

Hank DeBerry, the runner on third, scored easily. Dazzy Vance, who had been on second base, hesitated in his travels, figuring the ball might be caught. Finally, he lumbered to third base and rounded the bag. Then, fearing he would be cut down on a throw home, he retreated to third. Chick Fewster, the runner on first, had also hesitated, but finally headed toward third base. Herman never had any doubts that the ball would hit the wall. Head down, he sped around first base, then rounded second base and flew to-

AROUND THE BASES

ward third, a few feet behind Fewster. Now, seeing Vance go back to third, Fewster took a few steps in reverse. Herman ran past him and slid into third base. Fewster, thoroughly confused, turned around again and went to third. Three Dodgers were on the same base.

Which Runner Was Entitled to the Third-Base Bag?

Dazzy Vance, the fastballing pitcher who would eventually go into the Hall of Fame, deserved a good share of the credit for this mess. He should have headed for home plate instead of retreating to third base. But he was entitled to that bag. Where there's more than one man on a base, the lead runner gets it.

Which Runner Was Automatically Out?

Babe Herman was officially erased—no tag needed—once he passed Chick Fewster on the base paths. When one runner passes another, the man who does the passing is automatically retired.

What Should Fewster Have Done?

Fewster was still alive as a runner and should have tried to get back to second base.

The baseball wound up in the hands of Eddie Taylor, the

YOU BE THE UMPIRE!

Braves' third baseman, but he was just as confused as the runners. Taylor tagged Vance and Herman, the two Dodgers he had no need to touch since one was entitled to third base and the other was already out. But he never tagged Fewster.

Assuming a double play had been made to end the inning (he saw two teammates being tagged), Fewster strolled toward his position as the Dodger second baseman. Now Doc Gautreau, the Braves' second baseman, realizing the inning wasn't over, got the ball and headed toward Fewster. Finally discovering he was still a live base runner, Fewster fled into right field. By running away, he was automatically erased for going outside the base paths, but Gautreau caught up with him anyway and tagged him on top of the head.

Could It Happen Again?

There's never been another case of three men on a base, but in Game 3 of the 1963 World Series between the Dodgers and Yankees, the descendants of the "Daffiness Boys" got two-thirds of the way toward emulating their forebears.

As in the Babe Herman snafu, it happened in the seventh inning. Los Angeles's John Roseboro was on third and Dick Tracewski on second with nobody out. Don Drysdale, the Dodger batter, grounded out, second to first. Tracewski ran to third base, only to discover that Roseboro was still there. Tony Kubek, the Yankee shortstop, got the ball and tagged Tracewski out.

The Yanks also have looked like fools on the base paths. Monte Weaver, a pitcher for the Washington Senators during the 1930s, would recall the afternoon at Yankee Stadium when home plate became a crowded intersection.

"I was in front, 6–2, or something like that and I think it was the next-to-last inning," he remembered years later.

"Gehrig singled and then Dixie Walker singled, and Gehrig went to second. Tony Lazzeri hit a long fly ball to right-center field, and Goose Goslin ran and ran and got it on the first hop. Cronin went out to relay the ball. Gehrig tagged up till he saw the ball wasn't gonna be caught, and then he started running. Meanwhile, Walker was practically at second base.

"They were both running, one right after the other one. Goslin made a good throw to Cronin, who made a good throw to Luke Sewell at the plate. Here comes Gehrig sliding in, and Sewell tags him out. Here comes Walker sliding in, and Sewell tags *him* out. Double play."

It may have been a lost afternoon for the Yankees, but the Dodgers prevailed in both of their misadventures. Babe Herman's drive (he really doubled into a double play) proved to be the winning hit in a 4–1 victory. And the Tracewski-Roseboro fiasco came in a 1–0 Dodger triumph.

The last word in all this comes from Babe Herman himself. Long after his baserunning blunder, he remembered how on two other occasions it was he who had been passed on the baselines. (Glenn Wright and Del Bissonette were the miscreants, both foul-ups coming on the 1930 Dodgers.) "I know I made my share of skulls," Babe admitted, "but I wasn't as bad as they said."

The Atlanta Braves, telecast around the country on owner Ted Turner's superstation, billed themselves as "America's Team" through the 1980s. But more often than not, they were the National League's tailenders.

Then everything changed in the summer of 1991 as a young Brave ball club charged from last place to first in the league's West Division.

On the night of Tuesday, October 14, Atlanta seemed on its way toward getting the edge in the National League Championship Series against the Pittsburgh Pirates.

With the series tied at two games apiece, Dave Justice led off the bottom of the fourth inning of a scoreless game at Atlanta–Fulton County Stadium. The twenty-four-year-old power-hitting outfielder—the league's Rookie of the Year in 1990—symbolized all that was finally going right for a long-ridiculed franchise. And now he would get on base through a bit of good fortune.

He hit a routine grounder to first baseman Gary Redus, but the toss to pitcher Zane Smith, who was covering the bag, went wild. Justice wound up at second base.

The next two batters were retired with Justice staying

put. Then Mark Lemke grounded a single to left field. Barry Bonds fielded the ball as Justice raced to third.

Justice stumbled as he rounded the vicinity of the third-base bag, then continued toward home, arriving without a slide just ahead of the throw. Umpire Bob Davidson gave the safe sign. Atlanta had taken a 1–0 lead.

But Frank Pulli, the third-base umpire, noticed that Justice had neglected one elementary task: He had failed to touch third base.

A video replay would show what Pulli saw: Justice's right foot went over the base while his left foot hit the dirt inside the bag as he stumbled.

Justice hesitated as he rounded the bag, seemingly considering the possibility of retracing his steps, but then he kept going.

"He had a thought in his mind that he missed third base," the umpiring crew would say later in a statement. "That was the tip-off right there—when he stumbled, took a step back toward third, and then broke for home."

What Call Should Pulli Have Made When Davidson Signaled Safe at Home?

Pulli did nothing—which was exactly the right move.

The '91 Pirates were led by their "Killer B's," the one-two batting punch of Barry Bonds and Bobby Bonilla. But now a less heralded "B" sprang into action.

"Jay can't jump, so when he got four inches off the

ground, I knew something was going on," Pirate bull-pen coach Rich Donnelly would recall.

Jay Bell, the Pittsburgh shortstop, had watched Justice run to third and saw that he missed the bag. Standing at third (Steve Buechele, the third baseman, had gone into the outfield for a possible cutoff play), Bell frantically tried to get the attention of catcher Don Slaught. He jumped up and down and waved his arms, shouting for Slaught to throw the ball to him.

Slaught couldn't hear Bell above the crowd noise and simply tossed the ball to Zane Smith on the mound. But Bell kept yelling and finally got the pitcher's attention. Smith threw the ball to him and he stepped on third.

Up went Pulli's arm in the out sign: Justice's run was erased.

When an umpire sees a runner miss a base, he is not supposed to make a call. It's up to the opposing team to complain, and it must do so immediately.

Justice claimed later that his right foot had grazed the third-base bag, but Jimy Williams, the Braves' third-base coach, thought that Justice had indeed missed the base and did not dispute Pulli's call.

How had Jay Bell come to be so watchful on a play he wasn't directly involved in? When he was back in Double A ball, he had missed first base one time and was called out. From then on, he vowed to watch for others who would be led astray by their haste. "I learned from my mistake," he explained.

Justice's mistake would become a major gaffe. The Pirates scored a run in the next inning on José Lind's single, and the game ended in a 1–0 Pittsburgh victory.

But Dave Justice wasn't the only member of the Braves' organization to have a night to forget. Ted Turner and his fiancée, Jane Fonda, were trapped with twelve other people for twenty minutes in a stalled elevator at the ballpark before the game.

"It's like opening night in the theater," Fonda remarked when everyone finally got out. "When you have a bad dress rehearsal, that means the show's going to be good."

It proved, however, to be an omen of a different sort for the Braves' fortunes that evening.

They called him "the kitten." As a slender rookie left-hander back in 1953, he'd been a teammate of southpaw Harry (The Cat) Brecheen on the St. Louis Cardinals. The cutesy nickname for the youngster was hard to resist.

By springtime 1959 Harvey Haddix was in a Pittsburgh Pirate uniform, and on the night of May 26 at County Stadium in Milwaukee he had a perfect game going that extended beyond nine lives. He had, in fact, pitched twelve innings without allowing a base runner.

By the middle of the thirteenth inning, the Pirates had 12 hits off the Braves' Lew Burdette, but the game was still scoreless.

YOU BE THE UMPIRE!

The bottom of the thirteenth proved unlucky for the thirty-three-year-old Haddix.

Felix Mantilla led off with a grounder to third baseman Don Hoak, whose throw went low and hit first baseman Rocky Nelson on the foot. Mantilla was safe. The no-hitter stayed intact but the perfect game had ended.

Eddie Mathews moved Mantilla to second base with a sacrifice and then Haddix issued an intentional walk to Hank Aaron in hopes of setting up a double play. That brought Joe Adcock, a strapping right-handed power hitter, to the plate. Adcock, who had struck out twice and grounded out twice, hit Haddix's second pitch—a high slider—to right-center field.

Bill Virdon, the center fielder, raced back and leapt, but the ball carried just over the wire fence at the 375-foot mark.

Mantilla crossed the plate on the apparent homer. Aaron reached second base but then headed across the infield toward the Milwaukee dugout on the first-base side. He thought the ball had landed at the base of the wall and that the game had ended at 1–0.

A jubilant Adcock, certain he had a three-run homer and oblivious to Aaron's misdirection, kept going. He was close to the third-base bag by time Aaron realized the ball had been hit out of the park.

AROUND THE BASES

What Was the Final Score?

The Braves' manager, Fred Haney, and his coaches frantically tried to get Aaron and Adcock back in their correct order on the base paths. They had both of them retrace their steps. Aaron ran back to second base and Adcock got behind him. Then they went to third base and home plate.

But the umpires were unimpressed. Although Adcock's shot cleared the fence, he was automatically out when he passed Aaron on the basepaths. Since Adcock had, in effect, passed Aaron between second and third base (Aaron was headed toward his dugout at that moment), Adcock was given a double.

Umpire Frank Dascoli allowed Aaron's belated run to score and ruled the game a 2–0 Brave victory.

The next day, Warren Giles, the National League president, confirmed that Adcock would be limited to a double, but he changed the score to 1–0. When a hit drives in the winning run, the batter and the runners are permitted to advance only far enough to bring the game to a conclusion unless the blow is a homer. Since Adcock had really hit a double—not a home run—because of the baserunning snafu, the game had concluded the moment Mantilla touched home plate. Aaron's run was not needed so it did not count.

But a home run would now be allowed in this kind of situation because of a rule change made during the 1970s. If a runner cuts across the diamond thinking that a home run has ended a game, he is automatically out for abandoning his trip around the bases. Even though the man slugging the home run would, in effect, pass that runner, he would be entitled to the homer providing there had been less than two out.

Harvey Haddix, the only man to throw a perfect game for more than nine innings, found little solace in having allowed only one run because of the Aaron-Adcock base-running blunder. But he didn't wind up empty-handed. The following month, the National League presented him with a gift to commemorate his feat—a silver tray and a dozen sterling goblets engraved with the play-by-play account of the perfect innings they represented.

"That," said a gracious Haddix, "will be a perfect remembrance."

Elmo Plaskett of the Las Vegas Stars was truly a man in motion after taking his cut in a California League game against Fresno on August 10, 1958. He hit a home run and then circled the bases twice.

Plaskett drove the ball over the fence in the second inning, then crossed home plate behind the lone base runner, Angel Figueroa. Suddenly, Plaskett realized he had forgotten something—he had never touched first base. Figuring that Fresno might have noticed, then would appeal to the umpire, who would declare him out, Plaskett started all over again.

He ran to first base from home plate once more, this

time touching it, then circled the bases for the second time.

Should Plaskett Get a Home Run for His Trouble?

After the home-plate umpire put a new ball in play, the Fresno pitcher, Tom Fitzgerald, placed his foot on the rubber and threw over to his first baseman, who stepped on the bag. Fresno appealed to Umpire Joe Flucry to call Plaskett out.

The umpire did indeed give the "out" sign. Las Vegas argued, but it did no good. The ump was correct. When the ball is "dead"—as it is after being driven over a fence —and the batter misses a base, he may return to retouch it only if he has not reached the next bag. Once Plaskett touched second base, there was no way he could legally correct his mistake in failing to have touched first base. He was now at the mercy of the Fresno team. By calling attention to his lapse, he did the worst thing possible. He should have stayed in the dugout and accepted congratulations, hoping that Fresno had accepted the homer without watching for missteps on the bases.

Two full revolutions of the basepaths proved to be one too many.

YOU BE THE UMPIRE!

Gary Johnson wasn't running in slow motion, but it took him an hour or so to get credit for a home run he hit. And even after that happened, there were complications to come.

Johnson, a first baseman for the Indianapolis Indians, came up in the ninth inning of a June 1964 Pacific Coast League game against the Denver Bears. Indianapolis was trailing by 7–1 and there were two men on base.

Johnson hit a drive to deep right field. The ball seemed headed for the stands, but it bounced back onto the field, having hit the fence in the opinion of Umpire Emmett Ashford. Johnson got to second base with a two-run double. The Indianapolis rally then fizzled and the game ended as an apparent 7–3 victory for Denver.

But after the game, Ashford learned that Johnson's shot had actually gone into the seats before caroming onto the field. So he ruled that the drive was a homer and the final score 7–4.

Could Johnson Keep His Delayed Homer?

It was hardly Johnson's fault, but he would be robbed of a home run—by the very umpire who had first given him a double, then changed his mind. For Ashford would reverse himself a second time.

The next day, Eddie Glennon, the Denver general manager, told reporters that the score had reverted to the original 7–3. Ashford remained convinced—albeit belatedly—that Johnson's drive had cleared the fence. But someone pointed out to him that Johnson hadn't gone beyond second base.

Johnson never touched third base or home because Ashford didn't let him do it—the ruling was originally a double. Nevertheless, the umpire decided that Johnson was legally if not morally remiss. So the double-turned-homer had turned back into a double and the final score would be exactly what it was the moment the game ended.

Gary Johnson would never make it to the majors. Emmett Ashford, however, would go on to better things. Two years later, he was promoted to the American League, becoming the first black umpire in big league history.

The 1963 New York Mets had few occasions for celebration. They weren't as bad as the original Mets of '62, but it's not easy to lose 120 games two years in a row. The '63 gang was routinely, rather than dramatically, dreadful. They finished at 51–111.

But Mets center fielder Jimmy Piersall didn't let the losing get him down. When he reached a milestone one afternoon against the Phillies, he cavorted.

In the first game of a June doubleheader at the Polo Grounds, Piersall hit the hundredth home run of his career. The homer, leading off the fifth inning against Dallas Green, was a typical Polo Grounds cheapo—a pop fly down the right-field line that glanced off the facade of the upper deck, 260 feet from home plate.

As Piersall rounded first base, he suddenly turned around and began moving in reverse. He made the rest of the trip back-pedaling.

Did Piersall's Showboating Sabotage His Homer?

The maneuver delighted the crowd of 19,901 and didn't violate the rules. So long as a batter touches the bases in the correct order while running out his homer, he can embellish his performance with whatever flourishes he likes.

But Piersall's theatrics were almost overshadowed by his teammates' collective efforts. In winning both games that day, the Mets climbed past the Houston Astros in the National League standings. They proudly claimed ninth place.

Bill Summers, a longtime American League umpire, once recalled the question fans most liked to ask him: "If a batter dropped dead while running out a homer, how would you rule?"

It almost happened back in baseball's dawn. James

AROUND THE BASES

Creighton of Brooklyn's Excelsior team, the game's first superstar, hit a tremendous drive in an October 1862 game against the Union club of Morrisania, now the Bronx. As he rounded first base, he collapsed in pain. But he got up again and managed to make it all the way around the bags. He was immediately taken to his father's home and doctors were summoned. Four days later, Creighton died of internal bleeding resulting from a ruptured bladder suffered while taking his home-run swing. He was twenty-one years old.

That's apparently as close as baseball has ever come to a fatality amid a home run. But in a minor league game in the 1920s, an umpire had to rule on what was essentially the question that fans loved to throw at Bill Summers. The ump was Summers himself.

The Pittsfield Hillies of the Eastern League had a colorful and combative third baseman named Gus Gardella, who relished arguments with umpires, delighting the home crowd with his histrionics. One afternoon, Gardella paid off a ten-dollar fine resulting from an ejection by dumping a thousand pennies on home plate.

But there would come another day when he wasn't smiling and when he looked to an umpire for help.

Gardella hit the ball over the fence in a game against New Haven, but slipped on a muddy patch of ground rounding first base and broke an ankle. He was clearly in no shape to run out the home run.

YOU BE THE UMPIRE!

Could Gardella Get a Homer Without Reaching Home Plate?

The New Haven manager, Wild Bill Donovan, was in no mood for charity. "How are you going to rule this?" he asked Summers.

"I'm going to allow his substitute to run out the homer," the umpire told him.

"I don't know whether you can do it," retorted Donovan.

In the midst of the arguing, Gardella proposed a courageous solution. "I'll crawl around on my hands and knees if I have to," he offered.

Though the ballplayer was no friend of the umpires, Summers stuck to his decision.

"What I said goes," he told the New Haven manager.

And so a substitute came in to run out the homer.

Strange as the incident was, Summers did not ad-lib. He was simply following the rule book, which says that if "an accident to a runner" prevents him from reaching a base he's entitled to, "as on a home run hit out of the playing field," then "a substitute runner shall be permitted to complete the play."

So Gardella would get a home run in absentia.

AROUND THE BASES

When an infielder is waiting to tag a runner—ball in hand—he's a target for mayhem.

Game 7 of the 1934 World Series between the Tigers and Cardinals provided the most celebrated confrontation at a bag.

Eldon Auker, the Tigers' starting pitcher in that game, would recall years later what happened when the Cards' Joe Medwick barreled into third base in the sixth inning, trying for a triple.

"Marv Owen, our third baseman, was a tall, skinny guy. He was like a bag of bones. I think he was six feet tall and weighed about 160 pounds soaking wet. Medwick was built like a wrestler—a chunky guy.

"The throw went into third way ahead of Medwick, and he went in high and hard with one foot in the air and caught Marvin's shoulder with his right foot—a spike went through it. Marvin held on to the ball, and they called Medwick out. Marvin was mad and took a shot at him, and they were on the ground with Marvin on top, which was a little ridiculous."

"When the inning was over, Medwick went to the outfield. The Detroit crowd was in an uproar anyway because we were losing, and they started throwing things at him. A lot of people had stayed out there all night, and they had their food with them—apples and bananas, and even bottles. It was just a regular shower.

"Finally, Judge Landis went out and he got Medwick and took him off the field."

167

YOU BE THE UMPIRE!

Medwick's removal by the commissioner seemed the only alternative to a riot, and since the Cards were romping by 9–0, he wouldn't be missed. But in trying to kick the ball out of Owen's glove, he was playing within the rules.

If a fielder is on the move when a runner crashes into him, it may, however, be a different story.

There's a great pictorial cliché: A shortstop or second baseman leaps into the air and fires the ball to first as a runner barrels in, trying to bust up a double play.

If a news photographer can't shoot something special for the next day's paper, there's always a flying fielder available for the lens.

But mayhem at second base proved to be much more than a photo opportunity late in the 1988 season when the Dodgers played the Giants at Candlestick Park.

Twenty years after Don Drysdale threw his record fifty-eight consecutive scoreless innings, another Los Angeles pitcher was running up an amazing string of zeroes.

Orel Hershiser was facing San Francisco the evening of September 23 with four consecutive shutouts behind him. He hadn't been scored upon in forty straight innings.

In the bottom of the third, with the game scoreless, the Giants got a rally going. José Uribe was at third base and Brett Butler on first. With one man out, infielder Ernest Riles came to the plate.

Riles hit a ground ball to second baseman Steve Sax, who flipped to shortstop Alfredo Griffin for the force-out. As Uribe headed for home, Butler tried to break up the double play and, in the process, end Hershiser's scoreless streak. But as Butler approached Griffin, the shortstop was moving to the right of second base, getting ready to release the ball. Instead of sliding into the bag, Butler went for Griffin and swung his arm into the shortstop's leg. Griffin got rid of the ball, but it sailed over first baseman Tracy Woodson's head as Uribe crossed the plate.

Should Uribe's Run Have Counted?

Drysdale's scoreless streak had been kept alive in its forty-fifth inning by Umpire Harry Wendelstedt's controversial call nullifying a hit-batsman with the bases loaded for the Giants.

Now history would repeat itself: Another Dodger pitcher would see a similar streak continue thanks to another hotly disputed ruling depriving the Giants of a run.

Base runners try to dump pivoting infielders all the time, to the eternal gratitude of those newspaper photographers, but Umpire Paul Runge decided that Butler had gone too far—literally.

Runge ruled that Butler had illegally interfered with Griffin's attempt to complete a double play. So the ump gave the Dodgers both the out on Butler at second and the out on Riles, the batter, at first, ending the inning. Hershiser's streak was intact.

"He went after the shortstop instead of the bag," Runge said later. "He went out of the baseline to break up the play. He must go to the bag."

The rule book says a runner can't leave the baseline "for

the obvious purpose of crashing the pivot man on a double play, rather than trying to reach the base."

But Runge did acknowledge that his umpiring crew had made a call like this one only four or five times that season.

Butler, a superb base runner, could hardly believe what had happened to him.

"I slid just like I always did," he said. "I've never been called out before. Everybody knew what Orel was trying to do. They thought we had a run."

Butler wasn't the only one stunned by the call.

"I was rubbing the ball and thinking, *Okay, the streak's over, we're down 1–0 and I've got Will Clark coming up,*" Hershiser would say after the game. "Then I heard Runge's call. I turned and saw it and then I ran to the dugout because I knew what it meant. I wanted to get in there as soon as I could so that he didn't change his mind."

The game continued at 0–0 until the eighth inning when the Dodgers' Mickey Hatcher hit a three-run homer off Atlee Hammaker, Hatcher's first home run of the season in 173 at-bats.

Hershiser went on to a 3–0 victory, then would pitch ten shutout innings against the Padres the following week (the Dodgers would lose in the sixteenth) and end the season with fifty-nine straight scoreless innings, one more than Drysdale had racked up.

Hershiser's scoreless string had stayed alive thanks to a seldom-seen call. But Drysdale couldn't complain. The call that kept his streak going was even rarer.

AROUND THE BASES

When the Phillies played the Expos at Veterans Stadium the night of May 29, 1991, it was Charlie Hayes's twenty-sixth birthday. But the Philadelphia third baseman was hardly in the mood for celebrating when he took the field. He went into the game having gone 0 for 30 at the plate.

Hayes had slugged a few homers on previous birthdays while playing in the minors, but this time he wasn't trusting to good-luck charms. He had spent the afternoon with his hitting coach, Denis Menke, trying to lengthen his batting stride.

In the fifth inning, the Phils' Dale Murphy led off with a double, his 2,000th career hit. Ricky Jordan singled him home to tie the game, 1–1, and then Darrin Fletcher walked. Up came Hayes, having extended his futility to 0 for 31 earlier in the game. Now he finally got a hit—infield variety. Expo third baseman Tim Wallach got his feet tangled trying to field a grounder off Hayes's bat, and the official scorer didn't have the heart to deprive him of a single. So Hayes's drought had ended and the bases were loaded with nobody out.

The next batter, Dickie Thon, hit a grounder to second baseman Delino DeShields that looked to be a double-play ball. DeShields flipped the baseball to Spike Owen, the Montreal shortstop, who pivoted after the force on Hayes. Now Hayes did the same thing that Brett Butler had tried—he barreled into Owen in an effort to break up

YOU BE THE UMPIRE!

a double play when the shortstop came a few steps off second base.

As Jordan raced home from third, Umpire Eric Gregg made the same kind of ruling that Paul Runge had when Orel Hershiser's streak was on the line: He called interference on Hayes and awarded Montreal a double play. But in that Dodgers-Giants game, the double play ended the inning as a runner came home. In this game, there were only two outs after Hayes and Thon were erased.

Was Jordan Allowed to Score?

Charlie Hayes's momentary joy at ending his batting slump would turn to renewed misery. Not only did he fail to legitimately break up a double play, but he cost his team a run.

Ricky Jordan had ambled over to the Phils' dugout after crossing home plate. But now his presence was requested back at third base. And Darrin Fletcher, who had been at second when the play began, had to return there.

When a runner is called for deliberate interference, the rule book says that "all other runners shall return to the last base that was, in the judgment of the umpire, legally touched at the time of the interference."

So even though Jordan was far from the scene of the mayhem, his run didn't count.

Jordan never got beyond third, since the next batter, pitcher Terry Mulholland, flied out.

The game went to the bottom of the eighth tied at 1–1.

AROUND THE BASES

Then the Phils' leadoff batter crunched a pitch from Montreal's Barry Jones. The ball landed in the lower deck of the left-field stands and Philadelphia went on to a 2–1 victory.

The ballplayer who'd deprived his team of a run by his baserunning had won the game. It would indeed be a happy birthday for the suddenly slugging Charlie Hayes.

Don Hoak, the Cincinnati Reds' third baseman, grabbed an easy bounder and tossed the baseball to the shortstop one April day in 1957.

Just another routine assist on a force-out? Not quite. For this was an extraordinary fielding play. Hoak was running the bases at the time, and the player he threw the ball to was wearing the uniform of the Milwaukee Braves.

It was the top of the first inning at County Stadium. Hoak was on second base and Gus Bell on first with one down. Wally Post hit a grounder toward shortstop Johnny Logan, who got set to start a double play.

But Hoak stopped on his way from second base to third and scooped up the ball with his bare hands, then flipped it to an astonished Logan.

YOU BE THE UMPIRE!

What Happened to Hoak, Bell and Post?

Hoak had broken up a double play without ever sliding into a pivot man. In a clever maneuver, he sacrificed himself so the Reds could keep their rally alive.

And he got away with it—he'd found a loophole in the rule book.

Back in 1957, the rules stated—as they do now—that when a runner is struck by a batted ball before a fielder has a chance to make a play, the base runner is automatically out and the batter is awarded first base. (He's credited with a single.) But there was nothing in the code of conduct to prevent a runner from foiling a double play by deliberately interfering with a ground ball.

Umpire Frank Dascoli ordered Hoak erased, but Braves pitcher Warren Spahn was still in trouble (Bell was now on second, Post on first)—with two down—instead of being out of the inning.

Spahn retired the side without getting scored upon and he went on to a 3–1 victory. But Hoak had succeeded in his little trick.

He'd never get away with it again. Warren Giles, the National League president, happened to be a former Reds executive, but he took no pride in Hoak's cleverness. Four days later, Giles ordered his umpires to call out both the runner and the man behind him on the basepaths when a potential double-play grounder is sabotaged. The American League, expressing equal indignation, also vowed to nullify any similar stunt.

The rules were later rewritten to deal formally with a

AROUND THE BASES

latter-day Hoak. Now, if a runner "willfully and deliberately" interferes with a batted ball "with the obvious intent to break up a double play," the ball is dead and both the runner and batter are automatically out. No other runner can advance and no one can score.

The afternoon of April 21, 1974, marked the seventeenth anniversary of Hoak's trickery. It wasn't exactly a national holiday, but another ballplayer would celebrate the occasion by recreating the play.

The Texas Rangers, facing the Minncsota Twins at Arlington Stadium, had the bases loaded with nobody out in the sixth inning. Toby Harrah—like Hoak an infielder—was the runner on second. When Jeff Burroughs hit a grounder toward shortstop, Harrah was struck by the ball.

It wasn't quite as bizarre as Hoak's maneuver, since Harrah didn't actually field the baseball. But Umpire Ron Luciano was convinced that Harrah had deliberately run into the ball to break up a double play, so he invoked the rule that Hoak inspired. Both Harrah and Burroughs were called out and the runner at third had to return from home plate.

The Twins went on to an 8–2 victory that snapped a five-game Ranger winning streak.

Don Hoak had outwitted the rule book, but Toby Harrah paid the price.

YOU BE THE UMPIRE!

When a suicide-squeeze works, the club that pulls it off takes bows for a dashing brand of play. When it backfires, it creates instant bumblers. One night in July 1989, the Yankees tried it, but everything seemed to go awry.

It was the bottom of the eighth inning at Yankee Stadium with New York leading Milwaukee, 4–1. Wayne Tolleson was the batter with one out. Bob Geren was on first base and Mike Pagliarulo on third. As the Brewers' Jay Aldrich delivered the ball, Pagliarulo broke for home plate. Tolleson bunted, but the ball went into the air. Aldrich grabbed the baseball on the fly near his shoetops and threw to first base, doubling up Geren. Pagliarulo, who never stopped running, crossed home plate before the third out was made. After completing the double play, the Brewers ran off the field.

Did Pagliarulo's Run Count?

Although the Brewers pulled off a nifty play, their baseball IQ came up short. Pagliarulo's run did indeed count, but he could have been retired as a "fourth out."

Milwaukee assumed that the inning ended without the Yankees getting a run, and the scoreboard operator concurred, putting up a zero for New York. There was no

176

further scoring in the game, and when it was over, the scoreboard read "Yankees 4, Brewers 1."

But Larry Barnett, the home-plate umpire, had allowed the run, and the official box score would list the result as a 5–1 game.

The Brewers could have nullified Pagliarulo's run if their first baseman, after doubling off Geren, had immediately thrown to third base, erasing Pagliarulo as well since he had left the bag before the baseball was caught by the pitcher. It's as if he had come home on a fly to the outfield without tagging up.

But this was an "appeal play." The umpire could not call Pagliarulo out for leaving the bag too soon unless the Brewers appealed before going to their dugout.

Since the Brewers had not appealed, and since their double play was not a "continuous" one (it didn't involve a force-out since Geren could have remained on first base), Pagliarulo was allowed to score because he reached home plate before the third out was made on Geren.

The rule book envisions a situation like this one. It reads: "Appeal plays may require an umpire to recognize an apparent 'fourth out.' If the third out is made during a play in which an appeal play is sustained on another runner, the appeal play takes precedence in determining the out."

After the half-inning ended, Barnett pointed toward home plate to indicate that Pagliarulo had actually scored. The official scorer and the reporters simply didn't notice the gesture, so it remained a secret run, known only to the ump.

YOU BE THE UMPIRE!

Barnett hadn't pointed before the Brewers left the field because then he would have improperly tipped them off to making a play on Pagliarulo at third.

Though the Yankees benefited from the Brewers' oversight, reliever Lee Guetterman was deprived of a "save" because of it. A pitcher is credited with saving a game if he finishes up with his team in front by three runs or less. Pagliarulo's run gave the Yanks a four-run margin.

A similar play occurred in a Pacific Coast League game between Spokane and Vancouver on August 4, 1958, resulting in two runs scoring on a sacrifice fly. With the bases loaded and one out in the third inning, Spokane's Jim Gentile (later a first baseman with the Baltimore Orioles) hit a ball down the right-field line, but Vancouver's Joe Durham made a leaping catch. The runner on third, Bill George, tagged up and scored. The man on second, Tom Saffell, was off and running before the ball was snared and crossed home plate just ahead of Durham's throw to his first baseman, Ray Barker, to double up Glen Gorbous, the runner at first.

The home-plate umpire, Sam Carrigan, ruled that the run counted. The Vancouver manager, Charlie Metro, argued, but later admitted that before leaving the field, his team should have put on an appeal play at second base since Saffell hadn't tagged up. Like Mike Pagliarulo of the Yankees, Saffell would have been a legitimate "fourth out" if the other team had known the rules.

Instead, Gentile was credited with two runs batted in and Spokane went on to a 4–3 victory. The run that shouldn't have scored turned out to be the game-winner.

AROUND THE BASES

A glance out at Comiskey Park's left-field greenery when the White Sox took their first turn at bat one June evening in 1957 might have signaled a portent of strange doings. Patrolling the grounds for the Yankees was none other than Yogi Berra. A broken nose he'd suffered in a game against the Indians the week before had forced Casey Stengel to switch Yogi from his accustomed roost behind home plate.

The bizarre happenings would come in the third inning, the scenes of the action not Yogi's new surroundings but third base and his more familiar territory.

Bobby Shantz, a little left-hander who'd enjoyed his peak years with the lowly Philadelphia Athletics, was on the mound for New York with a 2–1 lead. There were two men out and Minnie Minoso was aboard at first base.

With Sherman Lollar, the White Sox catcher, at the plate, Shantz threw a wild pitch. Minoso, a fast man, took second, then tried for third. Elston Howard, catching in place of the banged-up Berra, retrieved the ball, then pegged it down to Andy Carey. The throw arrived a split second too late, Umpire John Stevens signaling that Minoso slid under the tag.

Carey and Gil McDougald, the Yankee shortstop, stormed at Stevens, insisting that Minoso had been tagged in time. The umpire's unwelcome response was a demand that Carey give him the baseball. But the Yanks kept arguing, and while the debate raged, Minoso decided to complete his tour of the bases. He took off for home plate, noticing that Howard had not yet returned there. Seeing Minoso sprinting away, Carey took time from his disputations to throw the ball home. Shantz managed to cover the plate and made a swipe tag. John Rice, the home-plate umpire, gave the "out" sign.

The Yankees trotted to their dugout and the White Sox began to take the field. But now Al Lopez, the Chicago manager, emerged for a discussion with Rice. The home-plate ump then gathered his three fellow umpires for a more formal meeting.

What Should Have Happened to Minoso?

The opportunistic Chicago outfielder was sent back to third base. The ruling: When the umpire at third had demanded that Carey give him the baseball, "time" was automatically called. Minoso had no right to run home and the Yanks therefore had no right to tag him out.

The rule book says that when an umpire calls time, the ball is dead and "no player may be put out, no bases may be run and no runs may be scored." The only exception is that runners may advance as the result of something that automatically entitled them to move on while the ball was still alive—a balk, an interference call, a throw into the stands or a home run.

With Minoso back on third base, Shantz pitched once again to Lollar. Moments later, the inning ended on a strikeout.

AROUND THE BASES

In the following inning, the Yanks came out second best once again on an umpire's decision: Shantz was hit by a thrown ball after laying down a suicide-squeeze with the bases loaded, but was called out for interference because he failed to run within the three-foot lane.

The Yanks were not so angry, however, by the time the evening ended. They had lost their skirmishes with the umpires but won the battle of the scoreboard. The final: New York 3, Chicago 2.

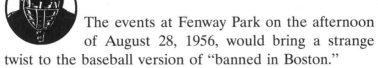 The events at Fenway Park on the afternoon of August 28, 1956, would bring a strange twist to the baseball version of "banned in Boston."

The Tigers were leading the Red Sox, 5–0, in the sixth inning with two out. Red Wilson, the Detroit catcher, came to bat with Bill Tuttle the runner at second. Wilson hit a grounder up the middle that was fielded behind second base by shortstop Milt Bolling. Tuttle tried to score and arrived at home plate together with Bolling's throw to catcher Sammy White.

White dived to make a tag but Umpire Frank Umont called Tuttle safe. Enraged by the call, White decided on an action that would speak louder than his words: He fired the ball in blind disgust toward second base.

Wilson, content with an infield single, was standing a couple of feet off the first-base bag at that point. Suddenly, he saw the baseball flying into a vacant patch of outfield. Jimmy Piersall, the center fielder, had come toward second base and was standing there with Bolling and second baseman Ted Lepcio when White's surprise peg whizzed past them.

Now Wilson started moving again. By the time Ted Williams had run the ball down from his left-field position, Wilson was well on his way toward home.

Standing at the plate was the still smoldering White. But the catcher, in a sense, wasn't really there at all. When White had thrown the baseball in anger, Umont did some throwing of his own—the umpire had tossed White out of the game.

Wilson completed his unexpected jaunt by crossing home plate before Williams could throw the ball home.

Should White's Ejection Have Stopped the Play Before Wilson Scored?

Umont allowed Wilson's run to count, bringing Dispute No. 2.

Red Sox Manager Pinky Higgins argued that once White was ejected, the ball should have been declared dead. "I told them we were playing with eight men," the manager said afterward. "White was out of the game, and if that doesn't stop the play, then what does?"

Higgins, who would join White in being tossed from the game—a 6–3 Tiger victory—claimed later that Umont himself had assumed the play was over before Wilson scored. The evidence? The ump had taken out his whisk broom and started to dust off home plate as Wilson approached. The Tiger runner had to wait for Umont to get out of his way before he could touch home.

But the umps insisted that play legally continued despite White's ejection because the catcher had kept the ball alive.

Explaining matters from his dressing room after the game, Umont reasoned this way:

"White was not thrown out of the game until he threw the ball. When he threw the ball, he put it in play and we couldn't call time until the play was finished. It didn't finish until Wilson crossed the plate.

"White is not out of the game the second he's ejected. If he had tagged Wilson, Wilson would have been out and then White would have left the game."

What about the little cleaning chore Umont had undertaken?

The umpire had seemed surprised to find Wilson bearing down on him as he stooped, his back to the mound, to do his touch-up job on home plate. But the umpiring crew contended that taking the whisk broom out does not mean that time is automatically out as well.

The moral of the story for aggrieved ballplayers: Ask for time out before throwing a tantrum—or a baseball.

YOU BE THE UMPIRE!

Pete Reiser was a sensation at age 22. He won the National League batting title as a Brooklyn Dodger rookie in 1941 and he could do it all—hit, run and throw. What he couldn't do was avoid outfield walls. A series of smashups turned a future Hall of Famer into a has-been by the end of the 1940s.

In the summer of 1973, now age fifty-five and already having suffered a heart attack, Reiser was mixing it up once again on a ball field. This time, serving as a coach with the Chicago Cubs, he was involved in a brawl at Candlestick Park. His afternoon ended with a familiar but unfortunate image: He was carried off the field on a stretcher.

Whitey Lockman, the Cub manager, was furious over Reiser's being kicked in the back of the neck by a San Francisco Giant player whom nobody could identify. But his anger went beyond that. He was enraged over a frolic on the base paths that the Giants' Dave Rader had taken in the midst of the melee.

The opening chapter came in the third inning when Giant pitcher Jim Barr, understandly irked at having given up a homer to Joe Pepitone—Barr's third home-run ball of the day—hit Ron Santo on the chest with his next pitch.

In the fourth inning, Barr came to bat and quickly saw what it was like on the receiving end: Cub pitcher Milt Pappas threw the ball in the general direction of his head.

Barr ducked, then took a few menacing steps toward the

mound. Both benches emptied, but the mayhem was confined to a shoving match between the Cubs' Jack Aker and the Giants' Chris Speier.

Suddenly, there was a man in motion—Dave Rader, who had been on first base with a single when Barr came to the plate. Deciding he'd rather run than fight, Rader had begun to circle the bases when tempers flared. Randy Hundley, the Cub catcher, retrieved the pitch that had sailed over Barr's head and threw to third as Rader arrived there. But there was no third baseman. Santo—the afternoon's first victim—had left his position to help his pitcher ward off Barr's anticipated fisticuffs.

The ball sailed into left field, so Rader sped around third and headed for home. Halfway there, he tripped over the Cubs' Cleo James—he, too, was running to the mound to join in Pappas's rescue—then continued on and crossed home plate.

Should Rader Have Been Allowed to Keep Going While Bodies Were Flying?

Home-plate umpire Augie Donatelli permitted Rader's run to count despite Lockman's claim that "time" should have been called.

Lockman argued that the field had become unplayable once it was littered with Cubs and Giants rushing out as reinforcements for the Pappas-Barr encounter. To bolster his plea, he noted that Rader had fallen over James, who wasn't supposed to be on the field. But the only thing this line of reasoning got Lockman was an ejection.

The way Donatelli saw it, the Cub catcher had kept things alive. "Hundley kept the ball in play by retrieving it and throwing it into left field," said the ump.

And if the ball is alive, so is the runner, especially if he keeps his head while everyone else is losing theirs.

Randy Hundley learned what Red Sox catcher Sammy White had discovered seventeen years before—the play isn't over until the umpires say it is.

Meanwhile, the fun wasn't quite over. Once everybody returned to their dugout seats, Pappas took aim at Barr again, this time plunking him on the right elbow. Barr flung his bat at the mound, everyone dashed out one more time, and poor Pete Reiser got blindsided.

Reiser was hospitalized as a precaution, but discharged the next day. At least he was no lighter in the wallet. Pappas was fined $250, his pitching teammate Jack Aker was docked $150 for some choice punches, and Manager Lockman was fined $50 for returning to the field after his ejection so he could partake in the second fight. Lockman turned out to be a three-time loser: He was thrown out, he was fined for throwing himself back in, and his Cubs wound up with an 11–9 defeat.

5

IN THE FIELD

The Japanese may have learned their baseball from America, but the derring-do displayed by an outfielder for Japan's Hankyu Braves back in 1981 should have awed even a Joe DiMaggio or a Willie Mays.

Masafumi Yamamori, the Braves' left fielder, raced toward the wall one day as a drive by the Lotte Orions' Sumio Hirota headed out of sight. At the last moment, Yamamori climbed the fence. He balanced himself on the wooden railing with his right hand and his left foot, then made a backhand stab of the ball.

A legal catch?

Here's one point where Japan and the United States are in agreement: Whether it's in Tokyo or Texas, a fielder can perch atop a railing if he's enough of an acrobat. The batter was out.

YOU BE THE UMPIRE!

Not only that, but the Japanese player's heroics were immortalized at the shrine to baseball U.S.A.: A photo of the catch was placed in the Hall of Fame.

The rule book has a lot to say about what is and what isn't a legitimate catch. What if a fielder falls into the stands after snaring the ball, then reemerges holding his trophy? What happens if a player catches the baseball, then drops it as he's about to toss the ball back? And suppose a fielder can't get the baseball out of his glove, so he throws glove—with ball inside—to his first baseman? The umpires and their trusty rules have the answers.

The Japanese may lay claim to baseball's most miraculous play, but American-style baseball can take credit for some of the game's more embarrassing moments.

Clay Bryant, a former pitcher for the Cubs, would recall a fielding fiasco he witnessed after he turned to managing.

"It was in Asheville, North Carolina—this was in '48, I think. It was a Sunday afternoon and we were getting beat, 10–2. The other club hit a ball to shortstop. The shortstop threw the ball over the first baseman's head. The runner started to second. My first baseman picked the ball up and threw it over the shortstop's head. The runner rounded third. My left fielder picked the ball up and threw it against the stands—it hit the backstop.

"It was very hot that day, and in the dugout we had a bucket of water with ammonia. I grabbed the bucket and ran out there.

"My catcher, a fella named Dayback, was ready to pick the ball up.

"I said, 'Don't you pick that ball up.' "

IN THE FIELD

"He said, 'What's the matter, skip?'"

"I said, 'That ball is too damned hot for you to pick up.' And I poured water on it."

Well, that was the low minors. But baseball's showcase event was the scene of an even more horrific fielding crime.

Hank Gowdy was catching for the New York Giants in the seventh game of the 1924 World Series against the Washington Senators. The game at Griffith Stadium was tied, 3–3, in the bottom of the twelfth inning.

With one out and nobody on base, Washington's Muddy Ruel lifted a pop-up behind home plate. Gowdy flipped off his mask and tossed it aside. But as he started after the foul, eyes looking up, something tugged at him from below. He had stepped on the mask. Gowdy hopped around, desperately trying to shake it loose, as the ball descended. Seconds later, it fell to the ground a few feet from the shackled catcher.

Given a second life, Ruel then doubled to left field. Moments later, the Giants were bitten by bad luck again. A ground ball hit by Earl McNeely struck a pebble and bounded over the head of third baseman Freddie Lindstrom. Ruel crossed home plate with the run that won the Series.

In its meanderings, the rule book even has things to say about the catcher's mask.

If a catcher corrals an errant throw by tossing his mask at the ball, the runners get an automatic two bases.

If a pitched ball becomes stuck in the mask, any runners can advance one base.

But if it's the catcher's foot that is stuck in his mask, it's simply a very bad day at the office.

YOU BE THE UMPIRE!

Ted Williams holds a slight edge on Jake Jones in career home runs: 521 to 23. But one afternoon at Fenway Park, Williams had to exert himself mightily for a homer while Jones managed to do almost as well by merely producing a dribbler.

The Red Sox were playing the Browns in a Sunday doubleheader in July 1947. In the sixth inning, Williams smashed a home run six rows into the center-field bleachers, just to the right of the 420-foot mark.

Moments later, Jones, the Boston first baseman, came to the plate against the Browns' Fred Sanford with two out and nobody on base. He hit a ball that traveled about 370 feet less than Williams's clout. The baseball bounded lazily outside the third-base line with Sanford in pursuit. Just to make sure the ball didn't change direction and roll into fair territory—giving Jones a single—Sanford threw his glove at it. He succeeded in deflecting the baseball toward the stands.

What Did the Rules Allow Jones to Do Next?

To his surprise and delight the Red Sox batter did not have to go back to home plate—he wound up on third base with a triple.

The rule book stated that if a fielder threw his glove at a ball and managed to deflect it, the batter had to be awarded three bases. No distinction was made between fair and foul balls.

The idea was to discourage an outfielder from hurling his glove in desperation when he was unable to run down a well-hit ball. (It's an automatic homer if a fielder throws his glove at a ball about to fly over a fence.)

The rule book hardly contemplated giving a batter a triple when he hit a squibber. But home-plate Umpire Cal Hubbard, citing the letter of the law, awarded Jones a three-bagger. Browns Manager Muddy Ruel, who happened to have a law degree, promptly pointed out how ridiculous the penalty was, but his argument got thrown out of Hubbard's court.

"Attorney Muddy Ruel, who can practice before the Supreme Court of the U.S., filed polite demurrers, hinted darkly about habeas corpus, ex–post facto and de jure, but nothing came of it," noted *The Boston Herald.*

Nothing further came of Jake Jones, either, in that inning—he was stranded at third.

The rule has since been changed. Now, if a fielder snares a batted ball by throwing his glove at it, the hitter gets a triple only if the scene of the crime is fair territory.

Jones would hit a total of five triples in an unremarkable career. But he will remain secure in his niche as the only man to get a three-bagger on a foul ball traveling less than ninety feet.

YOU BE THE UMPIRE!

The St. Louis Browns were the American League franchise most likely to succeed in deflecting batted balls with thrown gloves. Being perennial cellar dwellers, they were no strangers to desperation tactics.

Nine years before Fred Sanford's ill-fated glove-tossing, a Brownie outfielder had pulled the same maneuver.

The Cleveland Indians' Jeff Heath hit a long drive in the bottom of the ninth inning in a July 1938 game against the Browns that was tied at 7–7. Beau Bell, the St. Louis right fielder, hurled his glove at the ball in an attempt to slow it down. But by the time his glove struck the baseball, the winning run had crossed the plate.

How Many Bases Should Heath Be Awarded?

He showed a lot more muscle than Jake Jones would when the Red Sox batter was given a rules-aided triple against the Browns, but Heath got only a single.

In this case, the scoring rules took precedence over the rule requiring three bases. When a batter drives in a game-ending run, he is credited only with the number of bases he'd need to send that run across the plate unless he hits a homer.

Since the winning run came in before Heath even got to

second base, he was given a single and not a technical triple.

It was an episode truly worthy of the Browns. They had violated the rules, did not receive the maximum penalty, but lost the game anyway.

 Terry Mulholland brought the art of glove-throwing to unparalleled creative heights.

The rookie left-hander was down by 3–0 in the third inning pitching for the Giants against the Mets at Shea Stadium the night of September 3, 1986.

Having already yielded three hits and four walks, Mulholland didn't need any more trouble. And it seemed he'd caught a break when a ball slammed up the middle by Keith Hernandez landed in his glove on one hard hop. But then panic: As Mulholland reached to take the ball out and toss it to first base, it became stuck between the glove's middle and index fingers. The pitcher ran toward first, yanking at the ball, but it wouldn't budge.

So Mulholland removed the Wilson A2000 glove from his right hand and threw it—with the ball still inside—to first baseman Bob Brenly. The air-express package beat Hernandez to the bag.

YOU BE THE UMPIRE!

Was Hernandez Out?

Brenly now had two gloves and one baseball—not your orthodox arsenal. But after Umpire Ed Montague checked to be certain the ball was still nesting in Mulholland's traveling glove, he gave the "out" sign.

Score it putout by Brenly, assists by Mulholland and Wilson.

There was, however, one fielding ritual Brenly had neglected.

"I should have flipped thc glove around the infield," he noted.

Mets Manager Davey Johnson said afterward that he was going to argue, "but I didn't know what rule to bring up."

Shin guards, the mask and the chest protector had already been thought of, but the Orioles' Clay Dalrymple figured there would always be an idea or two whose time hadn't yet come.

One day back in 1969, the Baltimore catcher planned an innovation when he took the field: He had his regular mitt on his hand but a fielder's glove in his pocket. He would make a switch if there was a play at the plate, figuring the glove could more easily snatch a long throw.

IN THE FIELD

Was Dalrymple Too Much into Leather?

The umpires asked the catcher to put his experiment on hold until they got a ruling on the maneuver from American League headquarters.

Dalrymple would never get to enhance his leather wardrobe. The league vetoed the glove-and-mitt ensemble.

The rule book stated at the time that the catcher "may wear a leather glove or mitt." There was nothing specifically ruling out Dalrymple's scheme, but the rule-makers decided it violated the spirit of the law. "Glove or mitt" was not the same thing as glove *and* mitt, even if they weren't to be worn simultaneously.

The rule would later be changed in case any latter-day Dalrymples got bright ideas. Now it says that "the catcher may wear a leather mitt." The reference to a glove is gone.

In the 1950s, pitcher Bill Wight and catcher Joe Ginsberg of the Orioles worked out a scheme that foreshadowed Dalrymple's plan.

Their strategy: When Wight had to run past Ginsberg en route to backing up a play at home plate, they would make a trade. Wight would quickly give Ginsberg his glove and Ginsberg would give Wight his mitt. When the throw arrived at the plate, Ginsberg would have the best possible equipment for grabbing the peg and tagging the runner.

The stunt would be illegal if it were tried today, but the umpires back then didn't have to worry about a ruling. When the moment came to make the switch, Ginsberg couldn't get Wight's glove on. There was something they'd forgotten: The pitcher was left-handed.

YOU BE THE UMPIRE!

He was the nastiest of the Nasty Boys, and one night in July 1991, Rob Dibble would revive a violent baseball custom that went out of style even before the Civil War.

The Cincinnati Reds boasted a fearsome trio of relief pitchers in their 1990 World Series championship season. Dibble, Norm Charlton and Randy Myers could overpower and intimidate. They became known as the Nasty Boys.

The six-foot-four-inch, 230-pound Dibble had an explosive fastball and a temper to match. As the '91 season moved along, it was the latter that caught the headlines.

Dibble's troubles began early on. In a game against the Astros on April 11, he threw the baseball behind Houston's Eric Yelding, touching off a melee.

Seventeen days later, Dibble hurled the ball a lot farther. Angered with himself over a mediocre stint (he'd gotten a "save" against the Cubs but had yielded two runs in two innings), he threw the baseball from the Riverfront Stadium pitcher's mound into the center-field stands more than four hundred feet away. A female fan who surely had done nothing to offend Dibble was struck by the ball on the elbow.

When the Reds met the Cubs at Wrigley Field the night of July 23, Dibble had just returned from a three-game suspension for the Yelding incident. He was in the process of appealing a four-game ban and a thousand-dollar fine for hitting the fan with his spectacular throw.

Now Dibble's wrath would focus on a man hardly his size, the Cubs' Doug Dascenzo, a five-foot-seven-inch, 150-pound outfielder. In the eighth inning, Dascenzo put down a pretty squeeze bunt. As he ran to first base, Dibble revived the long-forgotten practice of "soaking."

Fielders were once allowed to retire runners by hitting them with thrown balls. The practice had been discarded as barbaric by the 1850s, but now it lived again.

Dibble picked up the bunt between the mound and first-base line, then saw he had no play on Chicago's Rick Wilkins, who was crossing home plate. So he ran five steps toward the line, planted his feet and then fired the baseball at Dascenzo, hitting him on the leg.

How Many Bases Did Dascenzo Get?

Where he wound up depended on two things—how resilient he was after being struck and how far the ball bounded away.

A runner may be awarded three bases if a fielder throws his glove at a batted ball. But if a runner is deliberately konked by a fielder, he gets no favors from the rule book.

While the umps can immediately eject a pitcher who intentionally hits a batter, there aren't any specific instructions for punishing a pitcher who, becoming a fielder, zaps a hitter after he's left home plate. And the player who's hit by the throw is not automatically given any bases.

YOU BE THE UMPIRE!

So Dascenzo was on his own, and he got to first base.

Home-plate Umpire Joe West, convinced that Dibble had deliberately taken aim at Dascenzo, did eject the pitcher. But National League President Bill White fined Dibble only $500—less than twenty percent of one day's pay—and did not impose what would have been Dibble's third suspension of the year. Later that season, another of the Nasty Boys would bare his testy side. In a September game against the Dodgers, Norm Charlton hit Mike Scioscia on the hand with a pitch in the sixth inning. It was no accident. Charlton later said he'd taken aim at Scioscia because he was convinced that the Los Angeles catcher, who'd reached second base three times, had been stealing the signs of the Reds' catcher from that vantage point, then relaying them to the batter.

The confession earned Charlton a seven-day suspension. It was a nasty penalty for the Nasty Boys' last hurrah of 1991.

When the Red Sox played the Cardinals in the opening game of the 1946 World Series at Sportsman's Park, Ted Williams found himself facing wide-open spaces on the left side of the St. Louis infield. Cardinal Manager Eddie Dyer sprang the baseball equivalent of football's unbalanced line. Dyer's first baseman, second baseman and shortstop were placed to the right of the second-base bag, and third baseman Whitey Kurowski was only a few feet to the left of second.

(Williams accepted the challenge, refusing to bunt or hit to the opposite field, and he went 1 for 3 with two walks.)

The Red Sox had no need to tilt their own infielders. In the bottom of the eighth inning, the Boston third baseman, Pinky Higgins, was playing where he normally would. But he became entangled with Kurowski—a runner this time—in a play that overshadowed the battle of wits involving Williams.

With two out and the game tied at 1–1, Kurowski singled to left. Joe Garagiola followed with a high fly to deep center field. The normally sure-handed Dom DiMaggio seemed ready to make the catch, but he was blinded by the sun. At the last moment, he reached frantically for the ball but it dropped safely.

Kurowski sped to third, but as he rounded the bag to head home, there was Higgins standing in his way. Kurowski had to grab Higgins and swing him around, then continued on.

Now DiMaggio retrieved the ball and threw to Higgins as Garagiola ran to third. Just before Kurowski crossed the plate, Higgins put the tag on Garagiola, and third-base Umpire Charlie Berry called him out to end the inning.

YOU BE THE UMPIRE!

Should Kurowski's Run Have Counted?

Home-plate Umpire Lee Ballanfant allowed the run, bringing Red Sox Manager Joe Cronin out of his dugout to protest.

"The first SOB who lays a hand on me is through," Ballanfant announced.

That kept the Red Sox from tagging the ump.

As for tags, Ballanfant knew that Garagiola was tagged before Kurowski reached home. Normally, that would nullify the run.

But that wasn't the issue this time.

Right after Higgins had blocked Kurowski's path, the third-base ump called obstruction on the Red Sox infielder. That meant Kurowski would automatically score. It didn't matter how long it took him to get to the plate.

Obstruction is called when a fielder "while not in possession of the ball and not in the act of fielding the ball, impedes the progress of any runner."

When Kurowski rounded third, Higgins wasn't ready to take a throw from DiMaggio, so he was guilty as charged.

In this type of play, the ball remains alive. So Garagiola was running to third at his own risk although Kurowski had been awarded home plate.

Boston went on to tie the game in the ninth, then won it in the tenth when Jimmie Foxx slugged a homer into the left-field bleachers off Howie Pollet.

"The Red Sox, who in their great years before 1918 had won five world titles without ever losing one, appeared

IN THE FIELD

headed for another and are heavily favored in the betting," *The New York Times* observed the next day.

Though the Red Sox overcame the call against them in Game 1, the optimism was a bit premature. Five decades later, Boston fans were still looking for that elusive World Series championship No. 6.

Eddie Montellanico, a nineteen-year-old right fielder for the Belmont Chiefs of the Western Carolina League, was set to catch a fly ball in a 1961 night game against Newton-Conover. Instead, the ball caught him—right on top of the nose. He lost the baseball in the lights and it bounced off his noggin and ricocheted over the fence. The batter, Newton-Conover's manager, Joe Abernethy, kept running.

Did Abernethy Get a Home Run?

Montellanico was knocked out cold. As for the baseball, it was knocked out of the park legitimately. It's a homer if a fly ball deflects off a fielder and goes over a wall.

But Montellanico got the last laugh. He was eventually revived and stayed in the game to see a 10–9 victory for his club. The next night, he had five straight hits as Belmont romped by 18–3.

YOU BE THE UMPIRE!

Now the scene changes from Carolina to Quebec and from the nose to the forehead.

In a May 1977 game at Olympic Stadium in Montreal, a drive by the Expos' Warren Cromartie struck the fence, bounced off the forehead of the Los Angeles Dodgers' Rick Monday, then went over the wall.

Did Cromartie Have a Homer?

If a baseball hits a wall or the ground before striking a fielder, then caroms over the fence, it's only a double. Monday lent a helping hand—or in this case a forehead—but because the ball didn't bounce off him on a fly, it's no home run.

The umpires had to make a decision quickly amid the pressure of a World Series. But the final word on their ruling would not come until forty-nine years later.

It was Saturday, October 10, 1925. A crowd of 36,493 bundled into overcoats and raccoon-skin jackets—among the spectators a frozen-faced President Calvin Coolidge—had turned out on a frigid, blustery afternoon at Washington's Griffith Stadium. The Senators, seeking their second consecutive Series title, were leading the Pittsburgh Pirates, 4–3, in the eighth inning of Game 3. Firpo Marberry, Washington's ace relief pitcher, had just entered the game, making his first appearance after missing five weeks with an injury. He struck out the first two batters to face him. Then Earl Smith, the Pirate catcher, sent a long drive to right-center field.

Sam Rice, an outstanding defensive player and at age thirty-five perhaps the fastest man on the Senators, had just been shifted from center field to right, replacing the slow-footed Joe Harris. Earl McNeely had gone to center.

Rice raced back and reached for the ball in front of a three-foot-high fence. Then he tumbled into the stands and disappeared for perhaps fifteen seconds. Finally, he scrambled back onto the field and triumphantly held the ball aloft.

Was Smith Out?

A fielder may reach over a fence to make a catch, but he does so at his own risk. If he falls into the stands and the fans jostle the ball from him, there's no interference. The seats are the spectators' sanctuary.

So the fact that Rice went into the bleachers did not nullify the catch. What the umpires had to decide was whether he dropped the ball and then had it returned to him by a fan.

The four umpires debated, and then Cy Rigler, who had been umpiring at second base and had the closest view, made the call. The catch stood. Rigler was satisfied that

YOU BE THE UMPIRE!

Rice caught the ball before going into the stands and that he never lost control of it.

Bill McKechnie, the Pirate manager, ran to the box seat of Commissioner Kenesaw Mountain Landis and demanded that he overrule the umpire. McKechnie argued that Rice had dropped the ball and that a sympathetic spectator had put it back in his glove. But Landis refused to dispute the umpires' judgment. Neither team scored again as Washington went on to win the game.

What had taken Rice so long to emerge from the stands?

The Pittsburgh team later located Pirate fans who had been seated in the right-field stands and were willing to provide affidavits that Rice dropped the ball but had it returned to him by a Senator supporter.

In the decades to come, Rice would never confirm he always had possession of the ball. "The umpire called him out," he would say. "The secret is more fun."

As skilled with the bat as he was with the glove—he amassed 2,987 hits in a twenty-year major league career—Rice would be elected to the Hall of Fame in 1963. But even then he refused to answer the question about the big catch.

Finally, after exhaustive prodding by Lee Allen, the Hall's historian, Rice agreed to provide his version of the play for posterity. On July 26, 1965, he wrote out a detailed account. The note was filed away by Paul Kerr, then the Hall's president, in his office at 30 Wall Street. Rice instructed that the letter remain sealed until his death.

Sam Rice died at age 84 on October 13, 1974—forty-nine years and three days after his controversial catch. In a suspense-filled ceremony soon afterward, Kerr slit open the Rice envelope and pulled out the letter.

It read: ". . . I turned slightly to my right and had the ball in view all the way, going at top speed and about 15 feet from the bleachers jumped as high as I could and back handed and the ball hit the center of pocket in glove (I had a death grip on it) . . . I toppled over on my stomach into first row of bleachers. I hit my Adam's apple on something which sort of knocked me out for a few seconds but Mc-Neely arrived about that time and grabbed me by the shirt and pulled me out. . . ."

Rice concluded: "At no time did I lose possession of the ball."

The umpires were vindicated—if Sam Rice is to be believed.

When the Portland Beavers played the Vancouver Canadians in a Pacific Coast League game the evening of Memorial Day 1991, it was a Vancouver player who proved to be the epitome of the eager beaver.

Rodney McCray was out in right field at Portland's Civic Stadium. He was an anonymous minor leaguer, recognized only when someone confused him with the pro basketball player of the same name. But by the following evening, the

YOU BE THE UMPIRE!

White Sox farmhand would be featured on baseball highlight shows throughout America.

A Portland batter named Chip Hale lifted a fly ball deep to right.

"I saw it and I started drifting back," McCray would recall. "The ball hadn't been carrying all night, but this ball just kept going. At first, I didn't think I was going to get to the warning track. The next thing I know, I'm at the wall. And the next thing I know, I'm going *through* the wall."

After the ball entered his glove, McCray exited the ball park. He crashed through a plywood billboard advertising the Nor-Pac frozen food company.

Could McCray Be Credited with a Catch?

The umpires would have given McCray a catch in absentia if they were convinced he held on to the ball after going through the fence. His leaving the grounds would be similar to an outfielder falling into the seats after catching a ball, à la Sam Rice. (One difference: If a fielder lands in the spectators' laps, the ball becomes dead and any runners on base are entitled to move up one bag if there is less than two out. If he stays on his feet upon exiting the ballpark, there is no automatic advancement for the runners.)

But McCray dropped the baseball upon leaving the grounds. What he picked up was a bloody nose and cuts on the forehead. But he was lucky to escape with only minor injuries. The Nor-Pac sign was one of three billboards on the Portland fence that could be popped in and out when workers needed to get from one side of the fence to the other. So it never splintered, but just dislodged in one piece. The next day, workmen put it back.

McCray wasn't the first outfielder to go through a wall. It happened in June 1930 at Lufkin, Texas, in a Class C Gulf Coast League game. Byron (Red) Ward, an outfielder for the Port Arthur team, made a leaping catch against a fence on a ball hit by Lufkin's Mel Carroll and then crashed through the wall. The runner on second, Patricio Lorenzo, headed for home plate. Ward returned to the field and threw to second, doubling Lorenzo off.

McCray did get some gifts from the frozen food company sponsoring the billboard and he was an instant celebrity. Above all, he was grateful to be in one piece.

"The first thing that came to my mind was, I thought about *The Natural* and *The Bingo Long Traveling All-Stars,*" McCray remembered. "They were two movies where guys ran through a wall. In *Bingo Long,* a guy named Esquire Joe goes through a wall and never comes back. And the guy in *The Natural* died. Me—I'm not dead, and I came back."

Terry Harper didn't climb over a fence in quest of a catch and he certainly didn't crash through a fence. He did have an unpleasant encounter with a bull-pen railing after snaring a fly ball on the run, and suddenly his glove was empty.

The Braves were playing the San Diego Padres at Atlanta–Fulton County Stadium on the next-to-last Sunday of the 1982 season. They were battling for a divisional title in a race with the Dodgers and Giants.

With Atlanta leading by 1–0 in the third inning, the Padres' Gene Richards, a speedy left-handed batter, came to the plate with two out and nobody on base. He hit a high fly down the left-field line. Harper raced to his right for the opposite-field drive and grabbed the ball while crossing the foul line. Third-base umpire Ed Vargo, running down the line, signaled the ball was fair when it touched Harper's glove.

Harper crossed into foul territory and then he stumbled for four strides. Suddenly he found himself at a railing separating one of the bull pens from the field. He grabbed the rail with both hands and lifted himself over. Just as that happened, the ball plopped onto the turf behind him.

Did Harper Make a Legitimate Catch?

The issue: How long must a fielder hold on to a ball after he snares it in order to be credited with a catch?

The rule book says "it is not a catch if, simultaneously or immediately following his contact with the ball, he collides with another player or with the wall or if he falls down and, as a result of such collision or falling down, drops the ball."

IN THE FIELD

What the rule book doesn't define is the term *immediately following*.

The umpire must decide that question.

Vargo ruled that Harper didn't have control of the ball long enough for him to be given the catch. Richards, who never stopped running, came all the way around to home plate.

"I didn't realize I had dropped the ball until I looked in my glove and saw it wasn't there," Harper said afterward. "Then I looked up and saw Richards running around the bases, and I thought: *What's going on here?*"

Seeing no "out" sign from the umpire, Harper leapt back over the railing, picked up the ball and threw it home. But Richards had already crossed the plate and the Padres went on to a 3–2 victory.

Then the official scorer made Harper even more unhappy, charging him with a four-base error. It was probably small consolation for him, but the National League office told the Braves the next day that if the official scorer didn't reverse himself, the league would erase the error and give Richards a home run.

The Braves lost a big ball game after the catch that wasn't. But over the next few days, there was no catching the Braves. They finished a game ahead of the Dodgers and two ahead of the Giants to capture the National League West title.

YOU BE THE UMPIRE!

Jack Clark's maneuvering in the Shea Stadium outfield one April night during the 1979 season was decidedly amateurish. But he had company. The umpires that evening were amateurs in every sense.

It took the umps twenty-eight minutes to decide whether Clark had made a legitimate catch, and they compounded the mess with a strange compromise that left both managers protesting the game.

The umpires for this Giants-Mets game were all from the amateur ranks—replacements for the regular umps, who were on strike in a pay dispute.

By time the first inning was over, even the most cold-blooded negotiator for baseball management must have been wishing for the real umpires' speedy return.

"The names are Bill Lawson, Phil Lospitalier, Merrill Hadry and Jerry Loeber," Red Smith wrote in his "Sports of the Times" column recounting the comedy. "With any luck they will someday take a place in the history of the labor movement right up there with Samuel Gompers, John L. Lewis and Eugene V. Debs. Wearing the plain blue serge of strikebreakers, the Messrs. Lawson, Lospitalier, Hadry and Loeber struck a mighty blow for the unemployed umpires of the major leagues the other night. A twenty-eight minute blow."

The Mets' Frank Taveras drew a leadoff walk, Richie Hebner singled him to third, and then Lee Mazzilli drove a ball to right field. Clark misjudged it as he backpedaled, seemed to catch the ball and then dropped it while drawing his arm back for the throw.

Taveras tagged up as soon as the ball touched Clark's glove and came home. Hebner went halfway to second base and then waited momentarily. When Clark seemed to have the ball firmly in his grasp, Hebner started back toward first. Then, when he saw the ball hit the turf, he started out for second again. Finally, he stopped once more, totally confused over whether the umpires were giving Clark the catch. Clark picked the ball up and threw it to Bill Madlock, the Giant second baseman, who stepped on first base. If there was a catch, then Hebner had been doubled off.

Phil Lospitalier, said to have been a high school and college umpire for twenty-five years, was working at first base. He decided the catch was good and ruled there was a double play.

Joe Torre, the Mets' manager, popped out of his dugout to argue that Clark had not, in fact, made a legitimate catch and that Hebner was therefore entitled to second base.

The umpires debated with Torre for five minutes, gathered in solemn conclave, and then reversed themselves: Clark had not made a bona fide catch after all, so Hebner was awarded second base and Mazzilli was allowed to take first.

Now Joe Altobelli, the Giants' manager, got in a few words of his own. Soon it was time for Umpire Summit Meeting II. The umps disappeared beneath the stands and sought the wisdom of Tom Gorman, the league's supervisor of umpires and a longtime ump himself.

While all this was going on, Vida Blue, the Giants' pitcher, busied himself with warm-up throws, not exactly the entertainment the 10,170 fans had come for.

After spending twenty-eight minutes pondering the problem, the umpires came up with a solution: Clark had made a proper catch, so Mazzilli was out. But Hebner was no longer a double-play victim. He could stay at first base because he had been confused by contradictory signals from one or more of the so-called umps. (The Mets went on to get four runs in the inning and won, 10–3.)

Could Clark Be Given the Catch Even Though He Dropped the Ball before Throwing It Back?

If a fielder catches a ball but then drops it in the act of throwing, the catch stands. The rule book says that "in establishing the validity of the catch, the fielder shall hold the ball long enough to prove that he has complete control of the ball and that his release of the ball is voluntary and intentional."

The key question is: How long is "long enough" to prove possession? That's a matter for the umpires' judgment.

What had surely gone on "long enough" in the spring of '79 was the umpires' strike.

IN THE FIELD

Apart from the ivy-covered walls, Wrigley Field is best known for its wind. When the gusts are blowing out, the baseballs rocket off the ivy, or over it, with devastating regularity as far as pitchers are concerned.

But on the afternoon of July 2, 1934, it was a catcher—and baseball's best-known umpire—who found themselves buffeted.

The Cubs were leading the Cardinals, 4–1, in the seventh inning. Chicago outfielder Chuck Klein was batting against Paul Dean with one out and the bases loaded. Klein was a slugger, but the best he could do was lift a pop-up behind home plate.

Bill Delancey, the Cardinal catcher, tried to get under the ball, but the winds carried it away from him. The baseball landed in fair territory beyond his grasp, and Klein landed on the first-base bag.

Was Klein Really Safe at First?

In dispute: Should the infield-fly rule be invoked?

When the bases are loaded or there are men on first and second with less than two down, the batter is automatically out when he hits a fair pop-up that an infielder can be expected to catch "with ordinary effort." The fielder does not actually have to catch the ball.

YOU BE THE UMPIRE!

The runners are entitled to retain their bases though they can advance at their own risk.

The aim is to protect the men on base. A fielder can not pretend he's going to catch the ball, then let it drop and start a double or triple play.

Bill Klem, umpiring at home plate in that Cards-Cubs game, refused to invoke the infield-fly rule. He contended that because of the winds, the ball could not be handled routinely.

Recalling the play years later, Klem would maintain that the pop-up "was buffeted about in the wind so much that the St. Louis infielders were lucky they weren't collectively skulled when it finally landed about twenty feet from home plate on the first-base side."

"Nobody in the St. Louis infield was ever in a position to claim he could handle the ball," Klem insisted.

After Delancey missed the catch, Cub pitcher Lon Warneke, the runner at third, made it to home plate.

The Cardinal manager, Frankie Frisch, Coach Mike Gonzales and Dizzy Dean (he wasn't in the game, but brother Paul stood to be the losing pitcher) argued with Klem that the infield-fly rule should have been applied and that Klein should therefore have been called out whether or not Delancey caught the ball. They also insisted that Warneke should not have been allowed to score, but their reasoning on that point wasn't too clear.

Klem rejected the Cards' argument, then ejected the three Cards who did the arguing.

The Cubs scored two more runs in the inning and won,

IN THE FIELD

7–4. The Cardinals immediately protested to John Heydler, the National League president.

Two weeks later, Heydler upheld the protest, deciding that the infield-fly rule should have been invoked and that Klein was therefore automatically out. But he allowed Warneke's run to count, figuring he would have scored anyway once the ball eluded the Cardinal catcher.

Heydler ordered that the game be replayed from the point after Klein's at-bat. He conceded that the infield-fly rule was "troublesome" and that the Cardinals may indeed have had problems making the catch, but insisted that "the batsman is automatically out when the ball falls within the infield."

The ruling was final, but it was also wrong. Nowhere does the rule book say that a pop-up has to land in the infield in order for the infield-fly rule to be in effect.

(Decades later, the rule would be invoked on a ball ultimately dropped by a left fielder. Larry Bowa, the Phillie shortstop, went back about sixty feet on a pop-up, and the infield-fly rule was called. Then outfielder Greg Luzinski shouted Bowa off. The ball hit Luzinski's glove and fell to the ground. But the batter was still out.)

Klem—a man of no small ego—remained bitter over Heydler's overruling him in what became a well-publicized incident. He would contend that Heydler caved in not on the merits, but because he was badgered by Sam Breadon, the Cardinals' owner.

Klem recalled that Heydler was at the game and "in my dressing room he assured me I had called it correctly. But Breadon's pressure became severe and Heydler asked me to admit that ball was an infield fly and I was wrong. After my fifth refusal he agreed officially that Breadon was correct and my decision was reversed."

Klem complained that St. Louis was not very sportsmanlike that day.

"The Cardinals were attempting to take advantage of the notoriously badly written" and "frequently ambiguous" rules, said Klem.

"They were written by gentlemen for gentlemen rather than by lawyers for lawyers," he maintained.

The Cardinal teams of the 1930s—featuring the Dean brothers, Pepper Martin, Joe Medwick and Leo Durocher—are remembered as the Gashouse Gang. Those ballplayers were colorful, tough and arrogant. Gentlemen they were not.

It looked like a simple fly ball for the Mets' Kevin McReynolds to snare. But the baseball wasn't the only thing soaring one Sunday afternoon at Shea Stadium in April 1987.

Just as the Atlanta Braves' Dion James led off the third inning by lifting a fly to left field, a dove was aloft. Ball and bird collided and feathers went flying.

Instead of landing in McReynolds's glove, the baseball ricocheted off the dove and nested on the grass yards away from the startled outfielder. By the time McReynolds caught up with the ball, James was on second base.

Should James Be Given a Wing-Aided Double?

There's nothing in the rule book that envisions a midair collision like this one, but it had happened before in the minor leagues so the umps weren't stumped.

The ruling: The ball remained alive although the dove was quite dead. If McReynolds had caught the fly, James would have been out. Since he didn't, the batter could get as far as his feet carried him.

"It may sound preposterous—we know God has other things to do—but we call it an Act of God," says Umpire John McSherry, who was working at first base that day.

The two batters following James were retired, so Mets pitcher Bob Ojeda would have been out of the inning if not for the mishap. But now Dale Murphy came to the plate with two out and James still on base. Murphy hit a homer to give Atlanta a 4–1 lead.

(It was fitting that a dove gave its life to help the Atlanta ball club, for the franchise was known as the Boston Doves in the early 1900s. There was no aviary angle here, however. The team was owned by the Dovey brothers.)

The dove was eventually picked up by Rafael Santana, the Mets' shortstop. He turned it over to a less-than-grateful ball girl, who brought it to her seat along the left-field line. At the end of that half-inning Ozzie Virgil, an

YOU BE THE UMPIRE!

Atlanta catcher on bull-pen duty, carted the dove away in a box.

"Birds usually do a good job of dodging balls," Virgil noted later. "But it ran right into the ball. Imagine. A dove. A bird of peace."

"I looked and saw feathers, then a bird falling," said Ojeda. "After this, I might go back and lock myself in my room."

Dion James, the recipient of good fortune, took a different view. "The bird died a hero to me," he said.

The most infamous encounter between ball and bird came the night of August 4, 1983, at Exhibition Stadium in Toronto. The Yankees' Dave Winfield, finishing his outfield warm-up tosses in the fifth inning, threw the baseball toward a ball boy near the Yanks' bull pen. A seagull—one of dozens visiting the park on a warm, foggy evening—was lolling on the right-field grass. The ball took one bounce and walloped it.

"Pow!" exclaimed Jeff Torborg, the Yankee pitching coach. "Right in the head. The bird went *pffft.*"

Winfield didn't endear himself to the fans when he held his cap over his heart as a ball boy removed the bird's remains with a towel. Fans in the grandstand tossed debris at him and shouted obscenities. After the game, Winfield had an encounter with the men in blue—but they weren't umpires. He was arrested and charged with cruelty to animals, a crime punishable by six months in jail. Unfortunately for Winfield, the victim of his accidental assault wasn't just any bird. The seagull, as a scavenger, is a protected species in Canada.

IN THE FIELD

Winfield was taken to a police station where he posted a five-hundred-dollar bond and was released. But before the week was out, a Toronto city official apologized for the arrest and the charges were dropped.

So Winfield avoided a six-month jail term in Toronto. He was, however, destined to serve six more years in the Bronx in the custody of his archenemy, George Steinbrenner.

6

WHO'S ON FIRST?

It was the youngster versus the old-timer when the Reds played the Tigers one day in April 1991.

On the mound for Cincinnati in the eighth inning was Tim Layana, starting his second season in the majors. At the plate for Detroit was a forty-six-year-old pinch hitter.

But it was hardly a case of an inexperienced pitcher cowed by a wizened veteran. For the batter had never appeared in a big league game and he never really would. It was the actor Tom Selleck, and the teams were at Florida spring training.

Previewing his role as an American player in Japan in the movie **Mr. Baseball,** *Selleck fouled off three pitches and then fanned on a curveball. End of act, end of major league career.*

Selleck was a pretender, but it doesn't take a make-believe ballplayer to produce strange doings in the lineup. Hitters have gone to the plate out of turn, managers have handed in botched lineup cards, and on one occasion the Philadelphia Phillies had a batting order that listed four pitchers just to confuse the opposing team.

There have been off-the-wall moments involving the lineup in the field as well. The Mets once pitched to a batter while their first baseman was lolling in the clubhouse. At the other extreme, the Pirates were accused one day of having ten men out there.

Arguments over personnel have even reached to the dugout. What if the owner suddenly decides he wants to be the manager? On a more democratic note, what if a ball club wants to let its fans run the team for a day?

Even the question of who can be seated on the bench has stirred a tempest.

The 1991 Reds didn't protest Tom Selleck's arrival at the plate, but a Cincinnati ballplayer vintage 1919 had a lot to say about an arrival in the opposing team's dugout one afternoon.

Jake Daubert, the Reds' first baseman, had been traded by the Dodgers the previous winter after filing a lawsuit against Brooklyn owner Charlie Ebbets in a pay dispute. When Daubert saw Ebbets sitting with his ballplayers during a game at Redland Field, he looked to baseball law for a bit of revenge.

The rule book says that "no one except players, substitutes, managers, coaches, trainers and bat boys" can be in the dugout.

Even back in 1919, the boss couldn't be one of the boys.

WHO'S ON FIRST?

Jake Daubert's son, George, would recall many years later how his father paid Ebbets back for reneging on his salary.

"My dad had the umpires chase him off the bench. So Charlie had to sit in the stands."

When Abbott and Costello argued over "Who's on First?" a baseball comedy classic was born. That very issue brought controversy and confusion one night in a game between the Mets and Astros at Shea Stadium.

Houston's Jeff Leonard had seemingly made the final out in a 5–0 Mets victory when he hit a fly ball to center field. But just before Pete Falcone delivered the pitch, Mets shortstop Frank Taveras had asked for time out, and Umpire Doug Harvey granted it.

The ball clubs left the field after Leonard was retired. But when Harvey told his fellow umps that the pitch hadn't counted, both teams were summoned back and Leonard returned to the plate.

The Mets' first baseman somehow didn't get the message. It wasn't Marvelous Marv Throneberry. This was August 1979, and although New York was in last place, the bumbling original Mets were a distant memory. The odd man out was Ed Kranepool, who in fact had gotten into three games with those 1962 Mets as a seventeen-year-old. By now he was an old-timer on the team, but when the clubs trotted back to the field, he stayed in the clubhouse, assuming his night's work was done.

Falcone resumed pitching to Leonard and got a couple of strikes on him, but then he singled. Now Joe Torre, the Mets' manager, ran out, finally noticing that Kranepool was nowhere in sight. He argued that Leonard's at-bat should be nullified once again, this time because the Mets had only eight men in the field.

Should Leonard's Single Count?

The rule book says "baseball is a game played between two teams of nine players each."

The umps held a conference, then reasoned that anything happening without nine men on the field doesn't count. So Leonard, having been retired, then having singled, was now ordered to bat a third time, and Kranepool belatedly came back to his position.

Before Leonard took his cuts again, another argument arose. Bill Virdon, the Astros' manager, insisted that Leonard should not have been deprived of his hit despite what the rule book said. Virdon pointed out it wasn't the Astros' fault that the Mets' first baseman had neglected to play first base. When Virdon lost that argument, he announced that the Astros were playing the game under protest. Meanwhile, he tried to make the best of the situation for Leonard's third at-bat of the inning. He argued that the strikes Falcone got on Leonard in his second at-bat should be wiped out since that entire time at the plate didn't count.

The umpires had another conference and agreed on Virdon's second point. Leonard resumed batting with the ball-and-strike count he was facing when his first at-bat had ended. Now he flied out to Joel Youngblood, the left fielder, and the game was finally over.

Not quite. The next morning, Chub Feeney, the National League president, who had been in the stands, upheld Houston's protest. He ruled that time had officially been in when Leonard batted with only eight Mets on the field, so New York's oversight should be overlooked. Feeney ordered the game replayed from the point where Leonard reached base.

Now it was Torre's turn, once again, to scream. "It's a shame that the sacred rules of baseball apply to everyone but a last-place club like us," he fumed. "Rule number one states baseball is a game with nine men on a team. Feeney's ruling stinks."

The league president had, indeed, contradicted the rule book, but he had the final say.

So hours later, Leonard was put back on first base and outfielder Jose Cruz came to the plate. Kevin Kobel, the Mets' starting pitcher for that day's regularly scheduled game, took the mound in place of Falcone. Now Cruz bounced out to second and the previous night's affair was history. The Mets had emerged with their 5–0 victory after getting the third out three times—first on Leonard's fly to center, then on his fly to left, and finally on Cruz's grounder. Pete Falcone had, however, been deprived of his complete game.

Why had Kranepool stayed behind when his teammates returned to the field?

"It wasn't my fault, it was the umps'," he maintained afterward. "I was here by my locker getting undressed after I saw the final out. Even Craig Swan told me the game was over."

Swan, one of the Mets' pitchers, wasn't in the lineup that night, so he may not have qualified as the highest authority. Yet Kranepool had one parting shot.

"They had to wait till I got back," he noted. "I guess they didn't miss me. Well, I won't miss them when I'm not here either."

He would not, in fact, be around much longer. The 1979 season turned out to be Kranepool's final year in the major leagues.

Six years after Ed Kranepool's disappearing act, another Mets first baseman was at the center of a dispute. Following a series with New York in July 1985, the St. Louis Cardinals complained to the National League office over the way Keith Hernandez positioned himself while holding runners on base. Hernandez would stand with his right foot touching the inside corner of the bag and his left foot across the foul line.

WHO'S ON FIRST?

Was Hernandez Cheating?

One of the slickest first basemen ever, Hernandez would win eleven consecutive Gold Glove awards. But he was a little too sly for the letter of baseball law. By positioning his left foot in foul territory, he was violating the little-known rule stating that "all fielders other than the catcher shall be in fair territory."

But Hernandez was hardly the only first baseman to cheat a little, and the umpires generally looked the other way.

Hernandez placed his feet so he could make a quick tag when the pitcher threw over to first. The maneuver also allowed him to shove off on his left foot to charge a bunt. All this was particularly annoying to the Cardinals, whose main offensive weapon that season was speed. They stole 314 bases in 1985, led by Vince Coleman's 110 steals.

After the Cardinals complained about Hernandez, the umpires warned him to toe the line—literally.

Gene Mauch had an arithmetic problem at Forbes Field one night in May 1964. The way the Phillies' manager saw it, the Pirates had the wrong number of players in the game.

The Mets would have one man too few against the Astros. The Pirates—according to Mauch—had one too many.

With the score tied at 4–4 in the sixth inning, Mauch noticed a familiar face in the left-field scoreboard: Elroy Face, Pittsburgh's ace relief pitcher.

Fearing that Face could steal the Phillie catcher's signs and then relay them to the Pirate batters, Mauch complained that the reliever was technically the tenth Pirate in the lineup. Since the scoreboard was in fair territory, so was Face, according to Mauch's logic.

Was Face an Illegal Extra Player?

Mauch told home-plate Umpire Bill Jackowski he was playing the game under protest. That prompted third-base Umpire Al Forman to investigate. But as Forman trotted down the line toward the scoreboard, the face—or Face— suddenly disappeared.

One inning later, Face was in the game for real, and this time he did nothing to anger the Phillies. He yielded three hits and one run as Philadelphia took a 5–4 lead. But Pittsburgh rallied in the ninth to win, 6–5, so Mauch submitted his protest to the National League president, Warren Giles.

Giles rejected the complaint, saying that Face had not violated the "spirit" of baseball law by being a theoretical tenth man. Being inside the scoreboard didn't really make him a fielder. And, said Giles, there was no evidence the pitcher's unusual vantage point had resulted in sign-stealing.

Face maintained after the game that he had a perfectly legitimate reason for being in the scoreboard. The reliever said he was seeking some relief of his own—he claimed to have been visiting the restroom on the board's ground floor.

"That's where we always go to the lavatory," he explained.

In the autumn of 1991, Ted Turner was in his baseball glory, tomahawk-chopping away with Jane Fonda as his Atlanta Braves miraculously made it to the World Series.

Turner was spurring his ball club on from the owner's box seat that October. But fourteen years earlier, under far less happy circumstances, he had assigned himself a vantage point even closer to the action—the manager's perch in the dugout.

Wallowing in a sixteen-game losing streak, the Braves were in Pittsburgh when Turner, who had bought the franchise the previous year, decided it was time for some on-the-job baseball education. He dispatched Manager Dave Bristol on a supposed ten-day scouting tour of the Braves' minor league system and anointed himself acting manager.

When the Braves took the field at Three Rivers Stadium

YOU BE THE UMPIRE!

on Wednesday evening, May 11, 1977, Turner was in the dugout, equipped with a minor amount of baseball savvy but a major league uniform.

Should Turner Have Been Allowed to Turn Manager?

The ultimate ruling on the boss's eligibility to be an employee would come not from the umps but their own bosses, the National League president and the baseball commissioner.

The umpiring crew let Turner have his day in the sun—or under the lights, as the case was—and the Braves didn't do too badly for a terrible team. They lost their seventeenth straight, but it was a 2–1 game with Dave Parker's third-inning homer making the difference.

Turner tried to look like a manager by shoving a wad of chewing tobacco into his cheek. Unfortunately, he couldn't figure out the correct order for putting on his pants, socks and stirrups.

He did not really push any managerial buttons. Vern Benson, the third-base coach, made the major decisions aided by Chris Cannizzaro, another coach, who kept Turner company in the dugout.

The owner did go on the field in the ninth inning, after the Braves' Darrel Chaney hit a drive that bounced over the fence for two bases.

Following the game, Turner was asked whether he'd been perplexed by the ruling on Chaney's shot.

"I know what a ground-rule double is," he said. "I may

be dumb but I'm not stupid. Only stupid thing I've done is buy the franchise."

Turner said he had left the dugout to make sure which player Benson wanted as a pinch hitter to follow Chaney. Perhaps the novice manager should have made the selection himself. The coach picked Rowland Office, who struck out to end the game.

Why had Turner taken over?

"Most businesses, you start at the bottom," he noted. "Here, unfortunately, I had to start at the top. What I'm really here for is to find out what goes on in the field and in the dugout."

Turner would have to do his learning quickly, because by the next day he was a former manager.

He had signed a standard coach's contract, but the following morning Chub Feeney telephoned to ask that he put his experiment on hold. The league president told Turner that baseball's administrative regulations (a code separate from the rules governing play) forbid anyone with a financial interest in a team from managing it unless the commissioner gave his approval.

That afternoon, presumably imbued with belated inspiration from a Turner pep talk the previous day, the Braves went out and finally won a game. With Coach Benson again making the decisions—this time unaided by Turner's moral support from the dugout—Atlanta ended its losing streak with a 6–1 victory over the Pirates.

Turner was not, however, ready to go quietly. He was hoping that Commissioner Bowie Kuhn would grant an exception to the rule cited by Feeney. (Feeney's invoking the regulation was actually a stalling tactic until Kuhn could act. The rule Feeney cited was aimed at barring a manager from owning stock in his team. It had not been adopted to prevent an owner from turning manager.)

In figuring out what to do about Turner, Kuhn was not exactly dealing with one of his favorite associates. The commissioner was involved at the time in a court fight over his effort to suspend Turner for violating rules on free agency in pursuing outfielder Gary Matthews, a battle Kuhn eventually won.

Now Kuhn quickly joined Feeney in telling Turner "gotcha."

"Given Mr. Turner's lack of familiarity with game operations, I do not think it is in the best interests of baseball for Mr. Turner to serve in the requested capacity," the commissioner huffed.

Turner did not take the rebuff gracefully.

"I don't know why I can't be with my troops," he said. "General Patton was on the firing line. What was it General MacArthur said, 'I shall return.' "

Instead, it was Dave Bristol who returned. When the Braves went home for a weekend series with the Cardinals, he emerged from exile to reclaim his manager's job.

Bristol had never gone on that minor league scouting expedition Turner cooked up. Instead, he'd retreated to his North Carolina home, humiliated and "bitterly disappointed" over being temporarily sacked.

Now Bristol would restore baseball wisdom to the Braves' dugout. But he couldn't manufacture good ballplayers. When the season ended, the Braves were where

WHO'S ON FIRST?

Turner could easily have taken them himself—in the cellar of the National League West.

Five days after he'd pulled the stunt of a lifetime by sending a midget to the plate for his St. Louis Browns, Bill Veeck summoned the "little people" en masse: More than a thousand fans were admitted free to Sportsman's Park to help manage the sad-sack ball club.

Veeck had advertised for a candidate to run the team on Grandstand Managers' Night and he received more than two thousand responses. One fan, Thelma Walker, wrote that the Brownies would be fleet of foot if she were at the helm. "They'd look at me and run."

Two local fans, Charlie Hughes and Clark Mize, were finally chosen to direct the team and were assigned to coach at first and third base. But American League President Will Harridge sent Veeck a telegram threatening a lifetime ban if he once again put an unauthorized person —whatever his height—in a Browns uniform.

So Hughes and Mize were assigned a box seat alongside the real manager, Zack Taylor, and his coaches. (Taylor had settled down before the game in a rocking chair atop the dugout, puffing away on a curve-stemmed pipe while lounging in bedroom slippers. But Umpire Bill Summers ordered him into the stands because he wasn't in his full uniform.)

YOU BE THE UMPIRE!

When the Browns took the field against the Philadelphia Athletics on the evening of August 24, 1951, a horde of 1,115 "grandstand managers" admitted for free was seated in the lower stands. (The total "paid" attendance was 3,925.) They were all given placards reading YES or NO.

During the game Bob Fishel, the Browns' publicity man, held up signs calling for decisions like BUNT, STEAL, or HIT AND RUN, and the fans would vote. A St. Louis judge named James McLaughlin quickly counted the yeas and nays, and then the decisions were relayed by Hughes and Mize via walkie-talkie to Johnny Berardino, a Brownie infielder who was coaching at third. (This bit of baseball show biz provided a wonderful start for Berardino's future career. He would go on to a long-running role as a doctor in the TV soap opera *General Hospital*.)

Did the Browns Break Any Rule by Bringing the Fans into the Game?

The league president and the umpires grudgingly allowed Veeck to go through with his populist promotion since the pennant was not exactly at stake—the Athletics were heading for a sixth-place finish, the Browns for the cellar. But the affair clearly ran afoul of the "fraternization" rule.

The regulation, which has occasionally brought small fines for violators, reads: "Players in uniform shall not address or mingle with spectators, nor sit in the stands before, during or after a game. No manager, coach or player

WHO'S ON FIRST?

shall address any spectator before or during a game. Players of opposing teams shall not fraternize at any time while in uniform."

The Brownie players went way beyond "mingling" with the fans: They took orders from them.

Charlie Hughes, the fan turned manager for a day, made a couple of lineup changes. He benched catcher Matt Batts in favor of Sherman Lollar and replaced first baseman Ben Taylor with Hank Arft.

The fans' first strategy moves came quickly. Ned Garver, the Browns' only good pitcher, gave up a three-run homer to Gus Zernial in the first inning and then allowed runners to reach first and third with one out. The grandstand managers were asked whether to yank Garver. They let him remain in the game and also voted to have the infield play in to cut off a run. But Garver asked the fans to consider playing the infielders back for a possible double play, and they agreed. Their willingness to be second-guessed paid off for St. Louis. Pete Suder hit a sinker ball into the ground, and the Browns indeed turned an inning-ending double play.

In the bottom of the first, the fans were asked whether Lollar should try to steal second with one out and a 3-and-2 count on Cliff Mapes. They said no, a wise decision. Mapes struck out on the next pitch, and Lollar, a slow runner, would no doubt have been erased.

Later in the inning, the fans grew bolder. With the Browns having tied the game, 3–3, they voted to have Arft —the man Charlie Hughes had put into the lineup—try to steal second. The Athletics, of course, could see the results of the voting, so they were hardly surprised when Arft took off. He was out by twenty-five feet.

Two hours later, the grandstand managers would emerge triumphant. Garver settled down and pitched all the way in a 5–3 St. Louis victory.

Jimmy Dykes, in his first season as the Athletics' manager, had threatened to protest the game if it took more than ten seconds for the fans to arrive at any decision. But Dykes's ill-humor received little sympathy from his boss. Among the grandstand managers, casting his own yes or no vote on Browns strategy, was the Athletics' ninety-year-old owner, Connie Mack. He'd retired as the Philadelphia manager a year earlier after fifty summers in the job and clearly missed having a say in strategy. In this case—fraternization rule or not—it was the opposing team's decisions he helped make.

As the Brooklyn Dodgers trudged to their dugout at the end of the fourth inning at Braves Field one April afternoon in 1931, their spirits were not exactly soaring. They were trailing, 8–0, and Babe Herman, for whom a fly ball was always an adventure, had already lost a couple of drives in the right-field sunshine.

When Manager Wilbert Robinson suggested to Herman that he latch on to something that day, Babe replied, "I can't catch what I can't see."

WHO'S ON FIRST?

"I'll put somebody out there who can see," snarled Robbie.

Robinson was planning to put Ike Boone—no flyhawk himself—in right field in the bottom of the fifth inning. Before that could happen, it came Brooklyn pitcher Les Mattingly's turn to bat, and Robbie put Boone up to swing for him.

When the Dodgers were retired, Boone trotted out to right field and Cy Moore was announced as the new pitcher.

Suddenly, Robbie started wondering where Herman was. He had forgotten that he had sacked him for the day and did not, after all, want to see the lumbering Boone out in right.

Enter Alta Cohen, a slightly built, curly-haired, twenty-two-year-old rookie, the son of a Newark, New Jersey, rabbi. Boone was yanked from the outfield and Cohen, making his big league debut, took his spot.

Where Should Cohen Have Batted in the Lineup?

Cohen was supposed to bat in the original pitcher's spot —number nine in the order—since Boone, the player he replaced, had pinch-hit in that slot. Moore, the reliever, was required to bat in Herman's number-three spot.

But nobody gave Cohen the message, and in the top of the sixth inning he came to the plate to lead off in Herman's spot. Outfielder Lefty O'Doul, in the on-deck circle, now heard shouting from the press box. "He's out of turn," a reporter yelled. O'Doul called time. "Are you sure you're right?" he asked Cohen. "I guess so," was the reply.

Cohen stepped into the batter's box and laced a single to left-center field. O'Doul batted next and was retired, and the inning proceeded with the Dodgers eventually scoring one run.

Should Cohen's Hit Count Even Though He Was in the Wrong Lineup Spot?

When a man completes an at-bat out of turn, it can be nullified, but the opposing team must notify the umpire of the mistake before any pitches are made to the man who follows the improper batter.

Once the complaint is made, the man who should have come to the plate is declared out. In this case, the proper number-three hitter—pitcher Cy Moore—would have been declared out and Cohen's at-bat would not have counted. Then O'Doul would have come to the plate with one out and nobody on base.

But the Braves' manager, Bill McKechnie, and their captain, Rabbit Maranville, didn't say anything during the sixth inning. So Cohen kept his hit.

In the seventh inning, the Braves finally awakened and notified the umpires of the mix-up. After a long conference, the umps shifted Cohen to the number-nine spot, where he should have batted his first time around. He hit another single in this inning, making him 2 for 2 in two different lineup spots. He also made a fine catch, and in the eighth inning he threw out two runners trying to stretch hits into doubles. The Dodgers lost, 9–3, and committed seven errors, "impersonating nine or more Marx brothers," as *The Brooklyn Eagle* put it, but Cohen had made quite an entrance.

The snafus weren't confined to the ball field. Quentin Reynolds, covering the game for the New York *World-Telegram,* wrote his story for the following afternoon's paper in the form of a letter to Cohen's mother. In those days, Western Union transmitted the reporters' copy from the ballparks to the newspaper offices. The Western Union operator took Reynolds literally and sent the story not to the *World-Telegram* but to the Cohen home in Newark.

Around 3 o'clock the next morning, Reynolds was awakened by a phone call from his office: "Where's your story?" It was finally tracked down at the Cohen residence and sent on its way to the newspaper.

The Dodgers had planned to demote Cohen to their Hartford farm club a few days later. But after his weird and wonderful debut, they decided to keep him awhile.

Before long, however, Cohen was shipped back to the minors and he played only a handful of games in the majors after that. Manager Wilbert Robinson, meanwhile, would not have too many more opportunities to botch his lineup order. The following autumn, after eighteen years in Brooklyn, he was fired.

YOU BE THE UMPIRE!

Before he replaced Connie Mack as manager of the Philadelphia Athletics, Jimmy Dykes had been the long-suffering manager of the Chicago White Sox, perennial also-rans in the 1930s and '40s. Dykes liked to needle Joe McCarthy back then by calling him a "push-button manager." Dykes's ball clubs were mostly a collection of mediocrities with the shining exceptions of Luke Appling and Ted Lyons. McCarthy's Yankee teams overflowed with talent. So Dykes let everyone know how he needed to work overtime using his brainpower while McCarthy simply pushed a figurative button and presto, a superhitter or pitcher would save the day.

But on the afternoon of August 1, 1932, McCarthy—actually a shrewd and highly respected manager—got his buttons all mixed up when the Yanks played the Tigers at Navin Field. (Later Briggs and then Tiger Stadium.)

In the pregame gathering at home plate, McCarthy gave Umpire Richard Nallin and Tiger Manager Bucky Harris lineup cards showing Ben Chapman, the right fielder, batting in the number-five spot and Tony Lazzeri, the second baseman, batting sixth.

Lazzeri had been hitting ahead of Chapman in the previous games, and in the second inning, it was Lazzeri, not Chapman, who came up in the fifth slot. But Lazzeri evidently had seen the lineup card and asked Nallin whose turn it should be. When the ump noted that the lineup card showed Chapman should be up, McCarthy emerged

WHO'S ON FIRST?

from the dugout. He claimed he had made a mistake and asked Nallin to allow him to switch the names. The umpire agreed. Lazzeri then hit a slow grounder to Heinie Schuble, the shortstop, who threw the ball wild. Lazzeri wound up on second via a single and an error.

Facing a ball club that had Lou Gehrig and Babe Ruth in the number-three and number-four spots, the Tigers needed any edge they could muster. So they complained that McCarthy should not have been allowed to make the switch.

The umpire decided that McCarthy's intentions took precedence over his penmanship and allowed Lazzeri's at-bat to stand. He said that a change from what was written on the lineup cards could be made if it was followed throughout the game. Now Chapman came up and got an infield single and then Frank Crosetti singled to score Lazzeri.

Bucky Harris announced he would protest the game if the Tigers lost. Lazzeri, hitting in the number-five spot all game, went on to get three singles and Detroit was beaten, 6–3. So the Tigers took their case to the league office.

Was Lazzeri's Disputed Single a Legitimate Hit?

The talents demanded of home-plate umpires do not include mind reading. No matter where McCarthy intended to have Lazzeri and Chapman hit, their batting-order spots as listed in the lineup cards were what counted. Or, in this case, what should have counted.

YOU BE THE UMPIRE!

Will Harridge, the American League president, ruled that Nallin should have gone by the official batting order. The rule book clearly says that no changes can be made after the ump gets the lineup cards.

So the Tiger protest was upheld and the game was ordered replayed on the Yankees' subsequent trip to Detroit. Actually, there would be two replays. The first one, part of a doubleheader, ended in a 7–7 tie called by darkness. The game was played for a third time the following day and the Tigers won it, 4–1. Joe McCarthy had pushed the wrong button this time, and it cost him a victory.

When the Braves played the Cubs at County Stadium one Sunday afternoon in August 1959, Milwaukee Manager Fred Haney was seeing double.

Chicago Manager Bob Scheffing had given Haney a lineup card showing Cal Neeman, the Cub catcher, batting in two spots: number six and number eight. Dale Long, the first baseman, was nowhere to be found on the card.

With the Cubs trailing by 1–0 in the seventh inning, Neeman—the man with the dual spot in the lineup—appropriately enough hit a double, batting in the number-eight spot. That put men on second and third with two out.

It was the moment Haney had been waiting for. He emerged from the dugout to demand that the double be nullified because of the snafu.

WHO'S ON FIRST?

Nothing had seemed amiss, however, to home-plate Umpire Tom Gorman. His lineup card correctly showed one Long and one Neeman. That card listed Long batting number six and Neeman batting number eight, and that's the way they'd come to the plate throughout the game.

Should Neeman's Double Have Counted?

Gorman allowed the double to stand, prompting Haney to play the game under protest.

The ump was right, but he was also wrong.

The rule book states that the lineup card in the umpire's possession "shall be the official batting order." So that's what the Cubs, the Braves and the umpires had to go by.

But Gorman should have spotted Scheffing's error when the lineup cards were exchanged.

The rules say that the home-plate umpire "shall make certain that the originals and copies of the respective batting orders are identical. Obvious errors . . . should be called to the attention of the manager or captain of the team in error. Teams should not be 'trapped' later by some mistake that obviously was inadvertent."

Haney, of course, was hardly "trapped." He could see Dale Long coming to the plate every few innings and was simply waiting for the right time to spring his own "trap," figuring he could take advantage of a technicality.

Though the Milwaukee manager lost the argument, his team won the game. The batter who followed Neeman— Irv Noren, hitting for pitcher Art Ceccarelli—popped up to end the inning and the Braves went on to a 2–0 victory. Because Haney was a winner, he would not carry through with a protest to the league.

Although Gorman wasn't reversed from on high, this was a day when he made everybody angry. As soon as the game ended, the Cubs' Scheffing ripped into him over the playing conditions.

Back in the fifth inning, with the Braves threatening to score, play had been held up by a rainstorm. The tarpaulin seemed to have a mind of its own, and by time the ground crew wrestled it down, the infield was a muddy mess. Nevertheless, after a delay of one hour and forty-six minutes, the game was resumed and the Braves quickly pushed across the afternoon's first run. But when the Cubs were threatening in the sixth, Ernie Banks hit into a mud-induced double play. The messy footing caused him to stumble coming out of the batter's box, turning what would have been a run-scoring force-out into a rally-killer.

"We should never have continued," complained Scheffing. "You had to hit the ball out of sight to get to first base."

By the end of the afternoon, it was Umpire Tom Gorman who was happy to be out of the sight of both managers.

WHO'S ON FIRST?

As the 1964 season neared its end, the Chicago Cubs were in their accustomed niche: the depths of the second division. Having locked up eighth place, they were looking toward next year. So when the Cubs played the Dodgers at Wrigley Field the afternoon of September 24 before a grand total of 629 fans—the smallest big league crowd of the year—Manager Bob Kennedy gave Ernie Banks the afternoon off. He put John Boccabella, a rookie just called up from Salt Lake City, at Banks's first-base spot.

But Banks was such a fixture in Chicago that Kennedy mistakenly wrote his name on the lineup card, leaving Boccabella's off.

In the seventh inning, Boccabella came up with the Dodgers leading by 3–1, one out, and Ron Santo on third base. Showing the kind of form displayed by the man he was replacing, he ripped a triple.

Dodger Manager Walter Alston now came out for a chat with home-plate Umpire John Kibler. Noting that the lineup card listed Banks, Alston asked that Boccabella's drive be nullified on grounds he batted out of turn.

What Should Have Happened to Boccabella's Triple?

Alston had decided to get an advisory opinion from the umpires early on. Back in the third inning, he instructed

YOU BE THE UMPIRE!

his shortstop, Dick Tracewski, to tell Frank Secory, the crew chief, that the Dodgers considered Boccabella to be hitting out of turn. Tracewski asked Secory what would happen if the Dodgers formally made an issue of the mix-up. The ump's reply: Boccabella would be considered an improper batter.

Boccabella was retired on his first two trips to the plate, so Alston held off from challenging him. When Alston finally complained after Boccabella's triple, Kibler ruled that the hit didn't count. Banks—considered to have been the proper batter though he never entered the game—was declared out under the scoring rules for lineup snafus. And Santo had to return to third base. Len Gabrielson then hit a grounder to end the inning.

Cub Manager Kennedy figured at the time that he had no argument. But during the next inning, Don Biebel, the Cubs' public relations director, phoned Kennedy and read another rule to him. That one said that "if no announcement of a substitution is made" (and mum was certainly the word on Boccabella), then the sub is considered to have entered the game if, as a fielder, "he reaches the position usually occupied by the fielder he has replaced, and play commences." The rule went on to say that any play made by such a fielder (or by a batter who steps into the box unannounced) "shall be legal."

So the Cubs would have had a case arguing that Boccabella was a perfectly legal player once the game began. But by the time Kennedy learned about the rule the umps had seemingly overlooked, it was too late to restore Boccabella's triple. And since the Cubs rallied to win the game, 4–3, they had no grounds for a protest.

But Ernie Banks did have cause to complain. Though he was warming the bench, he would be listed in the box score as having gone 0 for 1.

By time Banks's nineteen-year career with the Cubs had ended, he would compile some awesome statistics: 407 doubles, 512 home runs, 1,636 runs batted in.

He did it on 9,421 official trips to the plate. But the record book is not quite fair. For on a September day in 1964, Banks was charged with a time at bat when he was nowhere near the batter's box.

Left-handed catchers are as rare as managers who won't argue with umpires. But on June 29, 1961, the lefty-throwing Chris Short was listed in the Phillies' lineup behind the plate. There was nothing odd about Short being part of a battery. But he customarily did his job from the other end—he was a pitcher.

Short was a pawn in a managerial battle of wits between Philadelphia's Gene Mauch and San Francisco's Alvin Dark—a baseball chess game of sorts.

Neither man wanted to name his pitcher in advance, so in the moments before the game at Connie Mack Stadium, a total of five pitchers were warming up.

Each manager wanted to force the other one into a

lineup that would bring the best matchups for his pitcher: righty pitcher facing right-handed batters or lefty pitcher facing left-handed batters.

The home team has to hand its lineup card in first. Not knowing whether the Giants would start a righty or lefty pitcher, Mauch listed three of his own three pitchers in spots where he normally platooned lefty and righty hitters: Don Ferrarese was the center fielder and leadoff man, Jim Owens the right fielder batting number three, and Chris Short the catcher hitting number seven. Left-hander Kenny Lehman was listed to do what he normally did— pitch.

The Giants' starting pitcher turned out to be Billy O'Dell, a lefty.

When the Giants Came to Bat in the First Inning, How Long Would Ferrarese, Owens, Short and Lehman Have to Stay in the Game?

The first three Phils never had to take the field at all. The only person in the lineup who must actually see action is the pitcher—not one who is listed in another position but the hurler who is penciled in to be on the mound. The real starting pitcher—in this case Lehman—is required to dispose of at least one batter unless he is injured while pitching to that man.

Upon learning that lefty O'Dell was pitching, Mauch immediately sent three right-handed batters into the field to replace his three pitchers: Bobby Del Greco went to center for Ferrarese, Bobby Gene Smith to right in place of Owens, and Jim Coker behind the plate for Short, the pitcher turned phantom lefty catcher.

(The *Official Baseball Guide,* published by *The Sporting News,* would nevertheless list Ferrarese, Owens and Short as having played one game in the field during the 1961 season.)

The Giants loaded their lineup with right-handed batters against the left-handed Lehman. But that didn't faze Mauch. He had to leave Lehman in there for at least one batter, but he still had some relievers left. Lehman actually faced two hitters and then Mauch brought in the right-handed-throwing Dallas Green.

In the bottom of the first inning, Dark did some maneuvering of his own. O'Dell pitched to the required one batter, but then the Giants brought in the right-handed Sam Jones to face those righty batters Mauch had inserted in place of his out-of-position pitchers.

Mauch responded by juggling his lineup again. He put in two left-handed pinch-hitters, sending Tony Gonzalez up for Bobby Gene Smith and Clay Dalrymple to swing for Jim Coker.

The Giants went on to an 8–7 victory in ten innings. How was the game decided? Not by managerial brainpower, but simply power at the plate. Willie Mays—a man who would never be platooned—won it on his third home run of the day.

YOU BE THE UMPIRE!

In the first inning of a game on April 6, 1973, Ron Blomberg of the Yankees stepped to the plate against Luis Tiant of the Red Sox and drew a bases-loaded walk. Blomberg thereby became a footnote to baseball history: He was the first designated hitter. (For those devoted to more arcane trivia, he was also the first Jewish designated hitter.)

Since adoption of the DH by the American League, a debate has raged. The DH defenders argue that inserting a hitter in the pitcher's slot gives the fans what they want: more scoring. But in refusing to go along, the National League maintains that allowing the pitcher to hit—however puny his swings—retains a traditional element of the game. It also demands that the manager think: Should the pitcher sacrifice? Should he be removed for a pinch hitter?

But even when the designated hitter is used, there's room for scheming.

It was Billy Martin vs. Earl Weaver, a battle of wits between combative managers and creative thinkers, when the Yankees met the Orioles at Baltimore on September 5, 1976. At issue: a little-known section of the DH rule.

When Martin handed in the Yankee lineup card that night, his designated hitter was Cesar Tovar, who was in the leadoff spot. The Yankees' second baseman was Sandy Alomar, in the number-eight slot.

In the sixth inning, Alomar was scheduled to bat with two out and a runner on first base. But he complained of feeling ill and had to be removed. With the score 2–2, Martin did not want to use his best pinch hitter, Otto Velez, preferring to have him in reserve. So he ordered his pitcher, Jim (Catfish) Hunter, to hit for Alomar.

(In the bottom of the inning Tovar would be switched from designated hitter to second baseman, replacing Alomar and leaving New York without a designated hitter for the rest of the game. When the DH goes into the field, there can be no new DH.)

Could Hunter Legally Bat?

Even when the DH rule is employed, the pitcher who is in the game can eventually bat. But not the way Martin engineered it.

Umpire Marty Springstead permitted Hunter to hit for Alomar, but he was wrong. The pitcher is allowed to pinch-hit only for the designated hitter. That was Tovar, not Alomar.

Martin knew he was violating a rule, but got away with it.

"I told the guys on the bench, 'I don't think I can do this, but I'm gonna try it,' " he explained after the game. "If they told me I couldn't do it, then I would've put Velez up, but I wanted to save Velez for later. I was surprised Weaver didn't protest. I can't fault the umpire. When the hell did you ever see anyone do it? The guy who looks bad is Earl."

YOU BE THE UMPIRE!

The Orioles went on to win the game, but Weaver was embarrassed nonetheless.

"I didn't know the rule," he conceded.

Springstead admitted afterward that he made a mistake, but his conscience was clear.

The point in dispute—said the ump—was "a stupid rule."

7

BEYOND THE
BALLPLAYERS

During the World War II years, a fan's inalienable right to keep a baseball fouled into the stands was suspended by the demands of patriotism. Since the club owners were sacrificing for the war effort by letting the military take their prize talent, they figured that the spectators should also give something up. So the major leagues decreed that foul balls were to be returned to the field, then delivered to Army and Navy camps for recreational programs.

One day at Philadelphia's Shibe Park, a spectator decided that if he were going to lose his baseball, he would get something in exchange—an ump.

Soon after Umpire Art Passarella ejected the Athletics' third-base coach, Al Simmons, the fan hurled a foul ball back from the stands with gusto—he fired it in the vicinity of Passarella's head.

YOU BE THE UMPIRE!

In the old days, the fans were very much into the game. When ballparks were filled beyond capacity, the overflow would be herded behind ropes on the outfield grass. Ground rules would be devised for balls hit into the mob, and on more than one occasion the visiting team's outfielder tangled with an overly partisan gang.

In the truly old days, the sound of a click did not necessarily mean that bat had struck ball, at least so far as the Pacific Coast League went.

"Just as a fly ball was dropping into a fielder's hands, every gambler who had bet on the nine at bat would discharge a fusillade from his six-shooter in an endeavor to confuse the fielder and make him miss the ball," recalled Seymour Church, a nineteenth-century baseball historian.

Things are calmer now, but the fans do sometimes interfere with play. When that happens, the rule book is ready.

The coaches occasionally go beyond their boundaries as well. Third-base coaches have been straying from their boxes since Abner Doubleday laid eyes on the cow pasture where he didn't invent baseball. The rule book winks at a coach striding outside the chalk marks—it's okay if nobody complains—but it's another matter if he gets involved in helping a runner make his rounds.

The umpires, too, have gotten closer to the action than they're supposed to be. When they interfere with play, they must turn themselves in. There are rules to be invoked.

Every once in a while, an umpire will kick away a grounder he can't avoid. It's a turnabout of sorts. In the rough-and-tough old days, the umps were more likely to be on the receiving end of a boot.

BEYOND THE BALLPLAYERS

As Grantland Rice put it in his poem "A Tip to Teddy,"
advising Theodore Roosevelt to take up umpiring upon leav-
ing the presidency as a challenge equal to big-game hunting:

Chasing mountain lions and such, catching grizzlies
*   will seem tame.*
Lined up with the jolt you'll get in the thick of some
*   close game.*
When you hear Hugh Jennings roar, "Call them
*   strikes, you lump of cheese!"*
Or McGraw comes rushing in, kicking at your shins
*   and knees.*

Pitching before a crowd of 30,000 at Yankee Stadium one Sunday in July 1991, New York's rookie right-hander Scott Kamieniecki was in trouble. The California Angels had two men on base with one out in the second inning. But the batter he was facing, Luis Sojo, was a weak hitter, so Kamieniecki's chances looked pretty good.

Suddenly, however, the young pitcher was facing someone who had never signed a big league contract. It was Laurie Stathopoulos, a buxom twenty-four-year-old from Malden, Massachusetts, better known in certain circles by another name. She was Toppsy Curvey, an exotic dancer who'd been appearing nightly at the Fantasy Island club in

YOU BE THE UMPIRE!

Nyack, New York, and now had emerged from the stands to display her talents before a far larger audience.

Toppsy planted a big kiss on Kamieniecki's cheek, and he promptly dropped the baseball amid a sheepish grin. Seconds later, Toppsy departed in the embrace of security guards. Moments after that—perhaps still musing over his newfound friend—Kamieniecki delivered a fat pitch to Sojo, who rapped a two-run double down the left-field line. The Angels went on to an 8–4 victory.

The following night, Steve Howe was on the mound for the Yanks in relief against the Oakland Athletics. He, too, would become enmeshed in an incident where the central character didn't belong in the action, and, like Kamieniecki, he'd come unraveled.

The Yanks had battled back from a seven-run deficit to tie the game at 8–8. Howe was facing Jose Canseco in the eighth with one out and nobody on base. Canseco hit a hard ground ball that flew past Pat Kelly, the third baseman, and headed for the tarpaulin case down the left-field line.

Enter the ball boy. Apparently figuring the smash was foul, the youngster ran from his stool and made a one-handed grab of the baseball before the Yankee left fielder could reach it.

Where Should Canseco Have Wound Up?

Umpire Ted Hendry signaled interference and awarded Canseco second base. That brought Stump Merrill, the

BEYOND THE BALLPLAYERS

Yankee manager, flying out of the dugout. It was a decidedly less pleasant encounter than the one between Toppsy Curvey and Scott Kamieniecki. Merrill demanded that Canseco be given only a single. Hendry listened for a while, then demanded that Merrill take the rest of the evening off.

When a ballpark employee becomes involved in a play, the umpire must decide whether the interference was intentional.

If a ball boy (or ball girl, or park policeman) unintentionally interferes in the action, the ball stays alive. When a ballpark worker intentionally interferes, the ball is dead.

In determining intent, the umpire looks not at motives but deeds. The ball boy was not deliberately seeking to thwart Canseco. But by picking up the baseball, he intentionally became involved in the play. An example of unintentional interference would be if a park policeman tried to run from the scene of the action but was unable to avoid colliding with a ballplayer chasing a foul pop. It happened in an Astros-Braves game during the '91 season. The ball wasn't caught but interference was not called.

Hendry had no problem dealing with the matter of intent so far as the Yanks' ball boy went, so the ball was dead. Merrill was not arguing on that point.

What brought the fuss was the second decision the umpire had to make—how many bases to award Canseco. When the ball is dead because of intentional interference, the umpire must decide how the play would have developed had no interference occurred.

Merrill argued that because the ball was hit hard, Canseco would have been held to a single if the Yankee left fielder had had a chance to reach the baseball. But Hendry felt that Canseco would have had a double. So that's what the umpire gave him.

The next batter, Dave Henderson, drove a fastball to left field for another double, scoring Canseco with the tie-breaking run. Had Canseco been given only a single, there probably would have been runners on second and third.

By now Howe was thoroughly distracted. On the next play he committed a double error, permitting Henderson to score, and the Athletics went on to a 10–8 victory.

Pat Kelly, who had allowed the ball to get by him at third base on the disputed play, expressed anger afterward not at the ball boy but himself.

"I just messed up, took my eye off the ball," he said. "If they send the ball boy down to Columbus, then I should go down right behind him."

The ball boy was, in fact, headed for parts unknown moments after his gaffe. When the Yanks batted in the ninth, he was replaced by a presumably less-eager youngster. (Canseco, a more available target for the fans' wrath, was bombarded with baseballs and inflatable dolls hurled from the right-field seats when he took his position in the field.)

It probably didn't make the Yankee ball boy feel any better, but this wasn't the first time that someone in that kind of job had been dispensed with in a highly public manner.

In July 1986, the Chicago Cubs fired their twenty-eight-year-old ball girl, Marla Collins, who was in her fifth summer at Wrigley Field. Marla had become a popular local celebrity and had even gotten a contract to endorse athletic shoes. What did her in was too much exposure: She was sacked for posing nude in *Playboy*.

It was the case of the flying fan.

John Cangelosi, a speedy outfielder, led off for the White Sox in the eighth inning of a July 1986 game at Yankee Stadium. The score was tied, 1–1.

The left-handed batter had gone to the plate 31 times without a base hit, but suddenly his luck changed. He ripped a liner that first baseman Don Mattingly dived for but missed, and the ball bounded toward the low fence parallel to the baseline.

Right-fielder Claudell Washington pursued the shot, but as he closed in on the baseball, he had another object to contend with—a man who came tumbling out of the box seats.

Figuring that the fan had touched the ball when he leaned over, Washington switched to slow motion. He picked the baseball up casually and lobbed it to the infield.

But Mike Reilly, the first-base umpire, ruled that the spectator never got his hands on the ball.

YOU BE THE UMPIRE!

Did the Fan Interfere with Washington by Falling in His Path?

The ball is automatically dead if a fan touches it. There's no debate over intentional versus unintentional interference.

Yankee Manager Lou Piniella argued that the spectator had touched the baseball—a TV replay seemed to back him up—but both Reilly and home-plate Umpire Don Denkinger disagreed. In explaining his ruling afterward, Reilly said he didn't think the baseball was touched because "the course of the ball didn't change."

This play was not, however, disposed of so easily. The fan had been an unexpected flying object as Washington chased the ball down, and Cangelosi had gone all the way to third base after Washington gave up on making a play.

But the Yankees lost on that point too.

"The fan falling out of the stands does not constitute interference unless he interferes with the throw—and he did not," said Reilly.

The lesson for Washington: Assume nothing. Always play the ball.

If the Umpires Had Ruled Interference, How Many Bases Would Cangelosi Have Been Given?

The batter is usually given a double if a spectator leans over to grab a ball hit down the line.

Cangelosi, however, was no slouch on the base paths

even though his weak bat didn't get him there too often. (He would steal 50 bases that season.) And on this play, he received some help. When he was halfway between first and second, his alert third-base coach, Doug Rader, waved for him to keep going. By time the fan made his dramatic entrance onto the outfield turf, Cangelosi was steaming to third.

So even if interference had been called, "we would have probably had to put Cangelosi on third," explained home-plate Ump Denkinger.

Lou Piniella should not, therefore, have been too chagrined over losing his argument. Even had he won, Cangelosi would still have been at third.

That reasoning was, however, lost on the Yankee manager, who was still storming around when his ballplayers arrived in the clubhouse. The batter who'd followed Cangelosi—Ozzie Guillen—had hit a fly ball to center that sent Cangelosi home. It was the deciding run in a 2–1 game.

Three summers before, the White Sox had been on the losing end of an interference dispute.

With Chicago's Rudy Law on first base in the fifth inning of a game against the Orioles at Comiskey Park, Carlton Fisk hit a drive toward the left-field seats. Greg Kosc, the third-base umpire, signaled home run, but Oriole Manager Joe Altobelli claimed that a fan had leaned over the railing to catch the ball.

After a conference, the umpiring crew decided that Altobelli was right. Ruling that the ball would have bounded off the wall if the fan hadn't interfered, the umps gave Fisk a double and put Law on third base.

The White Sox's anger over the homer being disallowed was compounded by the umps placing Law at third. Chicago Manager Tony LaRussa argued that the speedy Law —he would have 77 steals that season—should have been awarded home plate since he would have come home had there been no interference. But the umps were unmoved.

Leading by 1–0 at the time, the White Sox never did score in the inning. The Orioles tied the game in the sixth, went ahead in the eighth, and wound up with a 2–1 victory.

LaRussa wasn't around to see the game unravel. He had been given the rest of the afternoon off by the umpires upon performing a most extraordinary base-stealing feat: After losing his argument back in the fifth, he'd picked up the third-base bag and heaved it into his dugout.

It seemed incredible that the White Sox's Dave Stegman had the energy to consider heading for home plate after chugging from first to third on a base hit. The White Sox and Milwaukee Brewers were staggering along in the twenty-third inning, their game having passed the seven-hour mark.

But Stegman was hardly exhausted. He was a designated hitter, so he'd spent most of the game sitting in the dugout.

BEYOND THE BALLPLAYERS

And the teams hadn't been playing for seven *consecutive* hours.

Their game at Comiskey Park, having started the evening of Tuesday, May 8, 1984, was into its second night. An American League curfew suspended play at 1:05 A.M. Wednesday with the score 3–3 after seventeen innings. The players got some sleep, then returned on Wednesday evening to finish things before that night's regularly scheduled game.

With Stegman on first base and the game deadlocked at 6–6 in the twenty-third, Tom Paciorek delivered a hit-and-run single. Stegman hustled to third, then turned toward home just as his coach, Jim Leyland, was raising his hands signaling him to stop. Stegman did not run himself into an out—but he did run smack into Leyland, who seemed to help him to his feet.

What Should Have Happened to Stegman?

The Brewers' manager, Rene Lachemann, claimed that Leyland had illegally interfered with play by making contact with Stegman. Jim Evans, the third-base umpire, talked things over with Ted Hendry, the umpire at first, who evidently had a better angle on what had happened. Hendry, agreeing that Leyland had aided Stegman, called the runner out.

It's interference when "the base coach at third base, or first base, by touching or holding the runner, physically assists him in returning to or leaving third base or first base."

White Sox Manager Tony LaRussa—his visions of an end to the marathon suddenly dashed—argued that while Leyland had touched Stegman, he had not done anything to help him get back to third base. LaRussa has a law degree, but it isn't in baseball jurisprudence. The umps were untouched by his argument.

(Asked after the game if he'd done anything illegal, Leyland would only say, with a nod toward LaRussa's office, "See my lawyer.")

The next batter, Vance Law, came to the plate with a runner on first instead of men at first and third. He singled to right, a hit that would have brought Stegman home with the winning run if not for the interference call. Instead, Chicago had two men on and nobody in.

The White Sox never did score in that inning and so the affair dragged on. It finally ended in the twenty-fifth when Harold Baines hit a 420-foot homer into the center-field bull pen off Milwaukee's Chuck Porter to give Chicago an 8–6 victory.

Among the records set in that two-night extravaganza:

—Longest game in major league history, 8 hours and 6 minutes.

—Most innings in an American League game, 25.

—Most innings played by a catcher in a single game, Chicago's Carlton Fisk, 25.

One record—held by few—had been tied:

—Most times causing interference to be called by touching a runner at the third-base coaching box, Jim Leyland, 1.

Bill (Brickyard) Kennedy was the Brooklyn Dodgers' top pitcher during the 1890s, but his mental powers hardly matched his physical assets.

Kennedy was illiterate and something of a rube. Once he set out from his Brooklyn home for a game at the Polo Grounds and wound up headed toward the Middle West instead. Finding himself lost on an uptown Manhattan train, he asked a policeman for directions, explaining that he was from Ohio and none too savvy about the big city. (His nickname derived from his hometown of Bellaire, Ohio, where brick-making was big.) The police officer thought Kennedy wanted to go back to Ohio and directed him to a railroad train bound for his home state.

So it's no wonder that a coach for the New York Giants figured one afternoon he could take advantage of Brickyard.

Kennedy and the Dodgers had a 2–0 lead going into the ninth inning of a game on August 1, 1897, in Brooklyn's Eastern Park. But the Giants rallied for three runs and had George Davis at second base.

The Giant players jumped up and down excitedly. But one man was thinking hard amid the hysteria. He was

YOU BE THE UMPIRE!

George Van Haltren, a Giant outfielder who was coaching at third base.

While Dodger catcher John Grim was arguing with Umpire Hank O'Day over the play that had just ended, Van Haltren ran down the baseline toward home plate. Kennedy, seeing the blur of a Giant uniform, thought it was Davis—the legitimate runner—who was trying to sneak a score. So he threw the ball home.

The baseball sailed past Grim—who was still occupied with his dispute—and now Davis got moving and sprinted across the plate from second base.

Did Davis's Run Count?

Van Haltren got away with his trick—the run was allowed. Not only that, but it proved to be the game-winner in a 4–3 Giant victory.

But if one of Van Haltren's descendants in the Giants' third-base coaching box tried a similar ruse today, the runner would be called out.

The rule book says it's interference if the third-base coach "leaves his box and acts in any manner to draw a throw by a fielder."

Brickyard Kennedy could not have felt very good the moment that ball game ended. But he would feel even worse afterward. The next day's *New York Times* reported that Bald Billy Barnie, the Dodger manager, had "fined Kennedy for his stupid work."

BEYOND THE BALLPLAYERS

Frank Secory was no stranger to handling batted balls. He played the outfield for five seasons in the big leagues, with the Tigers, Reds and Cubs.

But twenty-one years after his last game as a major league player, Secory encountered a baseball he wanted to avoid. This time he was wearing an umpire's uniform.

The Mets were playing the Cardinals at Shea Stadium on a Saturday afternoon in May 1967. Secory, umpiring at second base, was on the infield grass behind the pitcher's mound. New York's Jerry Buchek, who had doubled, led off second base as Ron Swoboda came to the plate with two out. Swoboda hit a sharp grounder toward Julian Javier, the second baseman. But before Javier could scoop it up, the baseball struck Secory on the leg. Then the ball caromed in the air and was grabbed by Dal Maxvill, the shortstop, as Swoboda reached first base.

While all this was going on, Buchek rounded third and headed for home plate. Then he became trapped in a rundown and was tagged out by Cardinal catcher Tim Mc-Carver.

Was Swoboda Entitled to First Base? Were the Cardinals Entitled to Tag Out Buchek Near Home Plate?

Both Swoboda and Buchek were still alive on the bases. A fair batted ball becomes dead if it touches an umpire before it has passed an infielder other than the pitcher. The baseball touched Secory before it got past either Javier or Maxvill. The only "fielder" it had bounded beyond was Nelson Briles, the pitcher.

Because the ball was dead, Swoboda got an automatic single while Buchek was required to hold at second base. Since Buchek had no right to head for home plate, the tag on him didn't count. The Mets were twice lucky.

Briles went back to the mound, presumably distracted and disgusted. Ken Boyer, a former Cardinal, now came to the plate and slammed the first pitch into the left-field corner for the three hundredth double of his career. Buchek took off for home again, and this time he made it, giving the Mets a 5–4 lead.

In the next inning, the Mets got four more runs, two of them coming when Buchek—still celebrating his good fortune—hit a double.

The game would drag on for three and a half hours and thirty-nine players would see action.

Did the Mets win?

Despite the aid unintentionally given them by Secory, and despite a grand-slam homer in the second inning by starting pitcher Jack Hamilton, they managed to bumble the game away.

St. Louis rallied for seven runs in the last three innings. Final score: Cardinals 11, Mets 9.

BEYOND THE BALLPLAYERS

It is twenty years later. Once again an umpire would become entangled in the action while the Mets were running the bases.

Darryl Strawberry opened the bottom of the second in an August 1987 night game at San Diego by drawing a walk from Eric Show. Kevin McReynolds struck out and then Gary Carter came to the plate. Strawberry promptly stole second and soon looked for more. On a 2–2 pitch, he tried to steal third base. As Umpire John Kibler signaled a called strike three, Padres catcher Benito Santiago fired the baseball to third baseman Chris Brown.

The ball sailed high and ticked off Brown's glove, carrying down the left-field line, as Strawberry slid. Seconds later, Strawberry was up again and he came home.

But Santiago had an excuse for throwing the ball wildly. Kibler had bumped the catcher's arm as he let the ball go.

What Should Have Happened to Strawberry?

After getting his walk Strawberry had done an impressive bit of running—270 feet worth. But he would wind up with only 90 feet gained.

Kibler called interference on himself for jostling Santiago and ordered Strawberry to return to second base. Not only was his run nullified, but the steal of third didn't count either.

YOU BE THE UMPIRE!

Mets Manager Davey Johnson argued, but he had no case. When the home-plate ump interferes with a catcher's throw, no runner can advance.

What if Santiago had thrown Strawberry out anyway?

The play would have counted. So either way, Strawberry couldn't get to third just yet. And he never did arrive there. The inning ended moments later with the game still scoreless and Strawberry left stranded.

The Philadelphia Athletics tried a fancy fielding play one July afternoon at the Polo Grounds back in 1913, but instead of getting the batter, they nailed the umpire.

The Yankees were up in the fourth inning with Roy Hartzell on second base and one man out. The batter, Babe Borton, hit a sharp grounder to the right of second base, where Eddie Collins made a nice stop. But Collins wasn't in position to throw to first, so he flipped the ball to Jack Barry, the shortstop. (They comprised one-half of the so-called "$100,000 infield," a wildly expensive group for that era that also included Home Run Baker at third base and Stuffy McInnis at first.) Barry wheeled and fired the ball toward McInnis.

It was all very clever, but what the Athletics hadn't anticipated was a daydreaming umpire.

Bill Dineen, the man in blue on the bases, was standing

270

a few feet from Barry on a line with first base. He forgot to duck. The ball hit the top of his head and bounced high in the air. It came down beyond the first-base line and rolled toward the stands. Hartzell had crossed home plate and Borton was on second base by the time the A's ran the baseball down.

How Far Should Hartzell and Borton Have Been Allowed to Advance?

Dineen may have been dead to the world for the moment, but the ball is supposed to remain alive on a play like this. Although a batted ball is dead if it hits an umpire before reaching a fielder, a pitched or thrown ball striking an ump stays in play.

So Hartzell should have been allowed to score and Borton was indeed entitled to second base.

But that's not the ruling Dineen made. After hearing arguments from the A's and Yanks, he called it a "do-over." Hartzell was sent back to second base and Borton was ordered to bat again.

Swinging away for the second time, Borton reached base on an error as Hartzell took third. Then Ezra Midkiff singled to left, scoring Hartzell and sending Borton to second. But Borton was stranded there, and the inning ended with the Yanks leading by 1–0. Had Borton been allowed to take second on the play the umpire botched, he would have come home on Midkiff's hit for a 2–0 lead.

The Athletics scored two runs in the sixth, the tiebreaker coming in on a throwing error by Borton, the Yankee first baseman, and the game ended in a 2–1 Philadelphia victory.

So Dineen's having lost his senses led to the Yankees' losing the game. The one run he cost them made the difference.

But the umpire may have had an excuse.

As *The New York Times* observed: "Big Bill had been standing in the hot sun for four innings and Jack Barry's carom off the umpire's head had plenty of speed, so perhaps Bill's head was badly muddled."

Bolstered by shin guards and chest protectors, well fortified with muscular physiques, catchers make for formidable obstacles at home plate.

But when the Cincinnati Reds' Bernie Carbo sped toward home in Game 1 of the 1970 World Series, Oriole catcher Elrod Hendricks wasn't his only problem.

Carbo had another roadblock to deal with: home-plate Umpire Ken Burkhart.

The score was tied, 3–3, at Cincinnati's newly opened Riverfront Stadium, the first ballpark to bless a Series with artificial turf. There was one out in the sixth inning. Carbo was on third, Tommy Helms was the runner at first.

Ty Cline swung on a 2–2 pitch from Jim Palmer and bounced the ball high in front of home plate. While Hendricks waited for the baseball to descend, Burkhart positioned himself on the third-base line, his back toward the third-base bag. He was in an excellent spot to determine if the ball came down fair, but he was also directly in the path of the onrushing Carbo, whom he seemed to have forgotten.

Carbo had almost reached home when Hendricks grasped the ball just to the right of the plate. With Burkhart blocking the base path, Carbo slid outside the foul line. But a collision couldn't be avoided. Carbo's leg hit Burkhart's leg and the ump started to fall down. Carbo slid past home plate, missing it to the outside because of his unsuccessful attempt to avoid Burkhart. As Carbo went by, Hendricks lunged in a bid to apply a tag.

What Effect Did Burkhart's Interference with Carbo Have on the Umpire's Call?

Unfortunately for the Reds, the blocking of home plate by the umpire was simply one more obstacle for Carbo. When a runner collides with an umpire, play continues.

The Reds didn't protest over Burkhart's being in the way. They were, however, enraged by his call: out at the plate.

Four towels came flying from the Cincinnati dugout, as did Manager Sparky Anderson.

The Reds claimed there was no way Burkhart could have seen the play since he was tumbling—his back to the action—while Hendricks was trying to make a tag.

YOU BE THE UMPIRE!

"He was looking straight at me when it happened," claimed Alex Grammas, Cincinnati's third-base coach.

Anderson maintained that if an umpire doesn't see a tag applied, he has to call the runner safe.

But Burkhart insisted he did see a tag. "I saw the play over my shoulders," he said. "I don't know how. It was a two-handed tag."

Video replays showed that Hendricks just missed Carbo with the catcher's mitt on his left hand. But even if he had made contact via the mitt, it wouldn't have mattered because the ball was in his right hand. And that hand—clearly shown in the replay holding the ball—was nowhere near Carbo.

And Carbo did eventually touch home plate. Although he missed it when sliding because of the entanglement with Burkhart, he unintentionally stepped on home when he sprang up to argue with the ump.

The decision was costly for the Reds. One inning later, Brooks Robinson broke the tie with a homer, and Baltimore went on to a 4–3 victory.

The previous October, the Orioles lost Game 4 of the World Series against the Mets when the umps failed to call interference at first base as a New York runner was struck by a thrown ball.

Burkhart hardly had that event in mind when he made his behind-the-back call, but it certainly seemed fitting that the Orioles finally got a break.

8

"THERE AIN'T NO RULE"

The image reappeared dozens of times at the drop of an umpire's decision: Going nose-to-nose with his nemesis, his feet kicking up dust, his jaw churning, his index finger stabbing the air, his cap askew, Earl Weaver personified the hell-raiser in spikes.

Having knocked around the minor leagues for twenty years as a five-foot-eight-inch infielder and then a manager, Weaver figured he had learned all the rules—and presumably how to break them—by time he took over the Baltimore Orioles.

Once he brought a rule book onto the field to bolster his argument. When the umpires told Weaver to take the rest of the day off, his rage intensified. Now the injustice was too much to bear. Weaver promptly tore the rule book to shreds in the umpire's face.

YOU BE THE UMPIRE!

"There ain't no rule that says you can't bring a rule book onto the field," he protested.

On occasion, a cunning ballplayer will try to make his own baseball law. A trick will be devised that is so inventive, there's no specific rule-book antidote at the umpire's disposal.

But even the most inspired maneuver can't outfox a determined ump. For the rule-makers have closed any loophole with a "gotcha" regulation.

It's what may be called the "no-rule rule."

Section 9.01 (c) of the "Official Playing Rules" states: "Each umpire has authority to rule on any point not specifically covered in these rules."

And sometimes the umpires must improvise amid a mess of their own making. In the rare situations where the umps botch things up, the solution may be nowhere in the rule book.

The old-time Umpire Bill Guthrie supposedly once remarked: "Dere ain't no close plays, me lad; dey is either dis or dat."

But baseball, like life, is not always so simple.

He was hardly a star at the plate or in the field, but his competitive fire could win ball games. He was known as "the brat," a ballplayer always looking for that little edge that could decide a game.

"THERE AIN'T NO RULE"

Eddie Stanky was the kind of player the equally combative Leo Durocher loved to have on his teams. In August 1950, playing second base for Durocher's New York Giants, Stanky was at his devilish best. The Giants were facing Boston at Braves Field. Bob Elliott, one of the Braves' top batters, was at the plate. But soon he backed out of the box, complaining that Al Barlick, the second-base umpire, was standing in his line of vision. Barlick moved out of the way. That gave Stanky a wonderful idea—he promptly moved into the way, standing in the spot the umpire had vacated.

Elliott shrugged off the harassment and hit two doubles in that game to help the Braves win. But Stanky was only beginning to perfect his routine.

Two nights later, when the Giants played at Philadelphia, he began waving his arms to distract Andy Seminick, the Phillie catcher, each of the four times he came to the plate.

Fuming over an "unsportsmanlike and strictly bush league" tactic, Eddie Sawyer, the Phillies' manager, protested to the umpires. In the pregame meeting the next afternoon, the umps asked Durocher to have Stanky halt his antics.

When Seminick came to the plate in the second inning, Stanky began waving his arms once again. But just before Sheldon Jones, the Giants' pitcher, went into his windup, Stanky froze. He was technically following the umpires' orders.

Seminick drew a walk, and soon he was heading for third base on a single, boiling with anger over Stanky's shenanigans. When Hank Thompson, the Giant third baseman, tried to tag him, Seminick let fly with an elbow. Thompson, an innocent victim, was knocked out cold. After five minutes, he stirred, then left the game and was replaced by Bill Rigney.

The next time Seminick came to the plate, the arm-waving truce was over. As reliever Jack Kramer went into his motion, Stanky began his gyrations again. Seminick responded by flinging his bat toward Stanky, and Umpire Lon Warneke responded by flinging Stanky out of the game. The charge: "conduct detrimental to baseball."

Durocher defended his ballplayer and was ejected as well, then announced he was playing the game under protest. When play resumed, Rigney was shifted to second base, replacing Stanky. Moments later, Seminick reached first on an error. Soon after that, on a force play at second, he barreled into Rigney, who came up swinging. Both benches emptied and a fine brawl erupted.

After the game, Durocher was still snarling in defense of Stanky.

"Smart ballplayers have been pulling stuff like that for all the twenty-five years I've been in baseball and it's perfectly legal as far as I'm concerned," he said.

"This is not Chinese checkers we're playing. No holds are barred on the ball field after one-thirty."

"I was just out there trying to help win a ball game," said Stanky. "If someone pulled that on me, I'd shake his hand and try to hit past him."

"THERE AIN'T NO RULE"

Was Stanky's Arm-Waving a Violation of the Rules?

"I do not want to discourage smart and aggressive play," said Ford Frick, the National League president, but "there are extremes, and baloney, and this was baloney."

There was nothing in the rule book that specifically barred Stanky from arm-waving, but Frick would take care of that little detail. First, he denied Durocher's protest over Stanky's ejection. Then he sent a telegram to his umpires instructing them to eject any player "who engages in antics on the field designed or intended to annoy or disturb opposing batsmen."

The edict eventually found its way into the rule book.

Rule 4.06 (b) says: "No fielder shall take a position in the batter's line of vision, and with deliberate unsportsmanlike intent, act in a manner to distract the batter."

Violating the rule brings automatic ejection.

Having succeeded in driving his opponents crazy, Eddie Stanky drove the rule-makers to rewrite the book.

Lenny Randle, playing third base for the Seattle Mariners, used considerable powers of persuasion in getting a ball to roll foul one night at the Kingdome in May 1981.

The Kansas City Royals' Amos Otis had topped the ball along the third-base line. Getting down on his hands and knees, Randle seemed to blow on the ball as Otis made it to first base. Slowly, the baseball changed course and rolled across the foul line on the infield's artificial turf.

Was It Quite Fair of Randle to Blow a Ball Foul?

The Royals' manager, Jim Frey, claimed that Randle had no right to blow on the ball.

For his part, Randle insisted he had done nothing of the kind. "I said, 'Please go foul, go foul,' " he claimed. "I did not blow on it. I just used the power of suggestion."

The home-plate umpire, Larry McCoy, now invoked his own considerable power. At first, McCoy threw up his arms to signal a foul ball, but after hearing Kansas City's complaint, he reversed himself and allowed Otis to take first base.

McCoy was convinced that Randle had indeed blown on the ball. There was nothing in the rule book that specifically prohibited a fielder from creating his own little jet-stream, but making a ball go foul without touching it is considered bad form.

This was a perfect situation to invoke Rule 9.01 (c), which gives the umps the power to decide on any point the rule book hasn't thought of. That's just what McCoy did.

Dave Phillips, the second-base umpire, said later that none of the umps working that night had ever seen a trick like Randle's.

"I think Lenny did it to be funny, and it *was* funny," said

Phillips. "But you can't alter the course of a ball. You couldn't throw dirt at the ball and get away with it."

Rene Lachemann, the Mariners' manager, took his ballplayer's word for it when Randle said he hadn't blown on the ball. But Lachemann was not so sure about Randle's claim that he'd cast a spell on the baseball.

The manager's conclusion: "Lenny said he yelled at the ball. The breath from his yelling must have moved it."

 In 1907 Roger Bresnahan of the New York Giants, a future Hall of Famer, became the first catcher to wear shin guards.

Eight decades later, a ballplayer named Dave Bresnahan followed in his great-uncle's path as a pioneer by introducing an innovation of his own.

The latter-day Bresnahan would hardly be remembered for his batting or fielding, but he'd become an instant folk hero. He was the first catcher to attempt a pickoff play without throwing a baseball—he hurled a potato instead.

It happened in September 1987. Bresnahan was catching for the Williamsport Bills, an Eastern League farm team of the Cleveland Indians, in a game against the visiting Reading Phillies.

Reading had a runner on third base. As the Williamsport pitcher was getting set, Bresnahan told the umpire he had a torn string on his mitt and he returned to the bench.

YOU BE THE UMPIRE!

A moment later, he came back with a new mitt. Inside it, he concealed a shaved potato.

Just before the next pitch, Bresnahan switched the potato to his bare hand. Then he caught the baseball in his mitt and fired the potato—intentionally hurling it wildly—in what seemed an effort to pick the runner off third.

Assuming that the white sphere he saw flying into the outfield was a baseball, the runner raced for home plate, only to be confronted by a triumphant Bresnahan, who tagged him.

Was the Duped Runner Really Dead?

The runner wasn't out. But Bresnahan was: out of the game and then out of a job.

The creative catcher would recall what happened as he completed his ruse:

"When I tagged the runner, the umpire looked stunned. He realized that the potato was in the outfield and called 'time out.'

"He said the runner was safe. I really thought they'd say 'do it over' like a net ball in tennis and get a laugh out of it. But the umpire didn't have any sense of humor about it at all. I think he thought I was trying to show him up. But I wasn't. I was just trying to put some fun into the game. I mean, it's not like it was the seventh game of the World Series.

"The ump said, 'You can't do that.'

"I said, 'Why not? What's the rule against it?'

"THERE AIN'T NO RULE"

"He said, 'You just can't do that. That's all.' I guess he was referring to his personal rule book."

But the issue wasn't really personal at all. Bresnahan was guilty on two counts. He had made a "travesty of the game" (a rarely cited no-no) and had been guilty of interference by duping the runner with an object that's not part of the game. Potatoes aren't an ingredient of the rule book.

The Williamsport manager, Orlando Gomez, immediately yanked Bresnahan from the field, and the club fined him fifty dollars. The next day, he arrived at the ballpark with a sack of fifty potatoes and left it with a message on the manager's desk. Borrowing a line from the Budweiser beer commercials, repeated ad nauseam as batters completed home-run trots, the note declared: *This spud's for you.*

Bresnahan was still at a low level in the minors at age twenty-five and was batting .149 in a part-time role. So he didn't seem to have a major league career ahead of him. Because of the prank, he didn't have a minor league career either. Soon afterward, the Indians released him from their organization. "You can't tamper with the integrity of the game," huffed Jeff Scott, Cleveland's director of player development.

Bresnahan, who had a college degree in business administration, went back to his hometown of Phoenix and turned to selling real estate. But the following Memorial Day, he was in his glory again. It was "Dave Bresnahan Potato Night" in Williamsport.

In a ceremony at the Bills' Bowman Field—the scene of

his crime—Bresnahan's number 59 was retired. It was painted along with his name inside a circle on the center-field fence. The mayor of Williamsport gave him the key to the city and fans were admitted for one dollar if accompanied by a potato.

Dressed in designer jeans and dinner jacket, Bresnahan recreated the play. The Bills' opponent that night was Reading, the team he had almost victimized. The man who had been on third, Rick Lunblade, was still with Reading. Once again he led off third base and once again Bresnahan fired a potato into the outfield.

After receiving a standing ovation, the hero made a little speech to the crowd of 2,734, Williamsport's second largest of the season.

"I remember a black-and-white film of Lou Gehrig when his number was retired," Bresnahan told the fans. "He said he felt like the luckiest man on the face of the earth. I feel luckier, because Gehrig had to hit .340 and play in more than two thousand consecutive games to get his number retired. All I had to do is hit less than .150 and throw a potato."

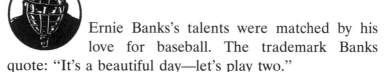 Ernie Banks's talents were matched by his love for baseball. The trademark Banks quote: "It's a beautiful day—let's play two."

On the afternoon of June 30, 1959, Banks wasn't playing

a doubleheader for the Cubs, but he was certainly seeing double. He was involved in a play where two baseballs were whizzing through the air simultaneously.

The Cubs were facing the Cardinals at Wrigley Field and Stan Musial was at bat in the fourth inning with one down and nobody on base. The 3-and-1 pitch from Bob Anderson was way inside and the baseball bounced toward the screen.

As Musial went down to first base, catcher Sammy Taylor ignored the ball in favor of arguing with home-plate umpire Vic Delmore. Taylor insisted that the ball had nicked Musial's bat for strike two. When the debate showed no signs of ending, Musial lit out for second base.

The baseball was picked up by Bob Schoenfeldt, the batboy, who tossed it toward Pat Pieper, the public-address announcer. But Cub third baseman Alvin Dark, who had rushed toward the backstop upon seeing Taylor otherwise occupied, intercepted it.

At that moment, Delmore absentmindedly handed a new baseball to Taylor. The catcher then gave the ball to Anderson, his pitcher, who had gone to home plate to join in Taylor's argument with the ump.

Now Anderson and Dark each noticed Musial heading toward second. Each was armed with a baseball and fired away.

Anderson's throw sailed over the head of Tony Taylor, the second baseman, and went into center field as Musial was sliding into second. Seeing the toss go wild, Musial got up and started for third base. Just then, Dark's peg arrived on the third-base side of second. Banks, the Cub shortstop, snared it on one bounce and applied a tag.

Should Musial Have Been Called Out?

An instant traffic jam was created as Cardinal Manager Solly Hemus, Cub Manager Bob Scheffing and players from both teams surrounded the umps.

Early in the debate, the umpires told Musial to return to first base, but after lots of finger-pointing and a couple of conferences, they called him out.

The Cards immediately announced they were playing the game under protest, but they went on to win, 4–1, so the protest was never filed.

Hemus said afterward that he would have based a protest on two points: First, he contended that the batboy had interfered with the ball. Second, he noted that Musial would never have tried for third base if he hadn't seen a baseball go flying into center field. That ball—the one tossed by pitcher Anderson—was the "second" one, and it should never have been put into play by the home-plate umpire.

"I didn't know there was a second ball in the game," Musial would say later.

Al Barlick, the umpiring crew chief, tried to give a coherent account afterward.

He said that the batboy's interference with the wild pitch was unintentional and so the baseball remained alive. Since it was that very ball that Banks was holding when he tagged Musial, the out counted. The second ball—the one Delmore had mistakenly given the pitcher—was never legally in play.

But Barlick overlooked two things.

Even though the batboy wasn't seeking to interfere with play, his motives were not what counted. The fact that he grabbed the baseball constituted interference in the eyes of the rule book. That should have caused the ball to be called dead with Musial awarded second base if the umps felt he would have gotten to that bag had there been no interference.

Barlick also ignored the fact that Musial was duped into trying for third base by Anderson's wild throw with the second baseball, which wasn't supposed to be anywhere but in the pocket of home-plate umpire Vic Delmore.

Having first donned a Cardinal uniform in 1941, Stan Musial had seen just about everything on a ball field. So he presumably could take this bit of craziness in stride. But when he reached base in the ninth inning, Cardinal Manager Hemus figured that Musial had seen enough action for one day. He sent Curt Flood in as a pinch runner.

 The bizarre Cardinals-Cubs episode was a case of déjà vu all over again, as Yogi Berra might have put it.

Not only had there been a two-ball snafu once before,

but it had happened at the same ballpark with two of the same men involved—Al Barlick and Bob Scheffing.

The Cubs were playing the Brooklyn Dodgers at Wrigley Field one July afternoon before an overflow crowd of more than 43,000, hardly the kind of turnout before which an umpire would want to embarrass himself.

The count went to 3 balls and 2 strikes on the Dodgers' George Shuba, and then the next pitch sailed high over the head of Scheffing, the Cub catcher. For a moment, home-plate ump Barlick inexplicably thought the ball had ticked the bat, so he reached into his pocket to hand Scheffing another baseball. That froze Scheffing, who was about to head for the backstop and chase down the wild pitch.

"He didn't foul that ball," said Scheffing, doing nothing to aid his own cause.

"No, no, he didn't," replied Barlick, quickly realizing he had blundered.

The mix-up gave Shuba a few extra seconds on the bases and he made it into second on the walk and wild pitch.

Where Should Shuba Have Wound Up?

Moments later, Barlick waved Shuba back to first base, figuring he would have stayed there if not for the ump's lapse that delayed Scheffing's pursuit of the ball.

That left Barlick with the unenviable task of facing Dodger Manager Burt Shotton. He went over to the Brooklyn dugout to explain how he was simply trying to find a fair solution, but Shotton was unimpressed and announced he'd play the game under protest.

The Dodgers went on to win it, 9–3, so Shotton didn't have to complain to the league office. As for Barlick, he was only warming up for the great two-baseball adventure to come.

For Walter Alston, it was as strange a play as he'd ever seen. That was going a ways, since Alston had been managing the Dodgers the night Umpire Harry Wendelstedt made his hit-batsman-that-wasn't call on Dick Dietz allowing Don Drysdale's 1968 scoreless-innings streak to remain alive.

But Alston wasn't alone in appreciating the weirdness enveloping Lee Lacy the night of June 19, 1974. Umpire Ed Sudol, who'd been in the big leagues for seventeen years, said he'd never witnessed anything like it either.

The Dodgers were at bat in the first inning, facing the Pirates at Three Rivers Stadium. Lacy was the runner at third, Jim Wynn was at second and Ron Cey at first base. There were two men out.

Joe Ferguson let a 3-and-2 pitch from Jerry Reuss go by.

Umpire Dave Davidson would later claim he yelled "ball" and that he'd never made a motion with his arm suggesting otherwise.

But both the Pirates and Dodgers heard—and even saw —differently.

Pirate Manager Danny Murtaugh said later that Davidson had yelled "strike." Pittsburgh catcher Manny Sanguillen said the strike call "was clear as a bell."

Assuming the inning was over, Sanguillen had rolled the baseball toward the mound and headed toward his dugout.

Lacy was sure he had seen Davidson gesture "strike," so he left third base and started toward his dugout to get his glove. "Everyone in the park saw him raise his right arm," Lacy would say.

Ferguson, the batter, said later that Davidson yelled something like "striball" and so he turned and asked the ump which half of the hybrid he liked best.

"He could have saved all the problems by pointing toward first base, but everyone was confused," said Ferguson. "It wasn't until I turned and asked him about it that he definitely said it was ball four."

So Ferguson trotted toward first base as Lacy went toward the Dodger dugout. Now Wynn, the man on second, realized that Ferguson had not been struck out but had walked. Seeing home plate unguarded and the baseball rolling to the mound, Wynn started running and he made it across home plate.

Then Lacy, Reuss and Sanguillen suddenly snapped to attention.

Lacy and Sanguillen both dashed toward home plate as Reuss ran out to the mound. The pitcher picked up the ball and threw it to his catcher. Lacy slid home—at a right angle to the baseline—just after the ball got there. Sanguillen applied the tag and Davidson called Lacy out.

Should the Inning Be Over, and If So, Do the Dodgers Get Any Runs?

The umpires held a conference to unravel the mess.

Their decision: Lacy, who had been called out at the plate, was allowed to score. Wynn, who had been safe at home, was really out.

The umps ruled that Lacy had been entitled to come home because of the bases-loaded walk. The "out" call on him by Davidson was a reflex action by the ump that didn't mean anything.

But Wynn was called out for having passed Lacy on the base paths, since Wynn had touched home before Lacy got there.

Lacy's run had technically scored after the third out had been recorded on Wynn. But there seemed no other solution.

"Our decision was strictly one of common sense," said Umpire Sudol. "Put all the components of that play together and you won't find it in the rule book."

Adding to the confusion, there was another element in dispute. Pirate Manager Murtaugh claimed that Lacy had entered the Dodger dugout before realizing he was wanted elsewhere and so had forfeited his right to return to the field. But the umps said they didn't see him go into the dugout. Lacy would insist he had never been more than five feet from the baseline. As long as he wasn't being chased by a fielder who had the ball, he was permitted to make his own base path, unorthodox as this one was.

But the fiasco would inspire a notation in the rule book —call it the Lacy clause. Now, a runner mistakenly "heading for his dugout or his position believing there is no further play" can be called out for abandoning his trip on the bases. The runner doesn't actually have to reach the dugout to be erased for misdirection.

Although the Dodgers got a run out of that mess, they might have been deprived of a big inning. If not for the mixed signal, they would have still been batting with a run in and the bases loaded.

In the fifth inning, Los Angeles lost out again on a decision by Davidson, who called the Pirates' Rennie Stennett safe at the plate on a close play. Pittsburgh would score four runs in the inning and go on to a 7–3 victory.

"That call hurt us more than anything else," said Alston later.

Maybe so, but there was one point in Davidson's defense: That time he definitely had no trouble making up his mind.

 By the summer of 1979, Lee Lacy had left the Dodgers. Now he was with the Pirates, the

"THERE AIN'T NO RULE"

ball club that had gotten a break when he strolled off third base back in June '74.

But even though Lacy had switched to a Pittsburgh uniform, he wouldn't be doing the team any favors. Once more an umpire would create havoc by misleading a base runner. That runner was none other than Lee Lacy.

It was the night of July 24 and the scene was again Three Rivers Stadium. The Pirates were trailing the Reds, 4–3, in the fourth inning with two out. Lacy was the runner at first base and Phil Garner was at third.

With the count 3 balls and 1 strike on Omar Moreno, Lacy set out to steal as Cincinnati's Fred Norman delivered the pitch.

Umpire Dave Pallone called "ball four," but Reds catcher Johnny Bench threw down to second anyway, saying later that he'd done so "instinctively."

Lacy slid into second, but he didn't beat the tag. Umpire Dick Stello gave the "out" sign.

Lacy didn't realize that Moreno had walked—entitling him to second base—and Stello didn't bother to give him that little piece of news.

Assuming he was erased—and the inning over—Lacy left the bag to get his glove. Then he saw Moreno starting to trot toward first base and it dawned on him that he wasn't dead just yet. He tried to scamper back to second, but Reds shortstop Dave Concepcion—who had originally tagged him on the steal play—applied a tag once again.

YOU BE THE UMPIRE!

Was Lacy Out?

The play took a few seconds, but the umpiring crew needed considerably more time to sort this one out: A thirty-four-minute argument followed.

The first part of the umps' ruling was easy enough: Because Moreno had walked, Lacy could not have been thrown out stealing despite Stello's call.

Now came the tough question: By not telling Lacy that the "out" call didn't count, had Stello improperly caused him to be tagged out afterward?

Pirate Manager Chuck Tanner would say later that Stello had admitted making a "mistake." But that was little solace for Pittsburgh—the umps allowed Concepcion's second tag to stand. Even though Lacy had stolen second, he was called out for wandering off the base without asking for "time."

The Pirates played the rest of the game under protest, and when they were beaten, 6–5, they complained to National League President Chub Feeney.

When Feeney's decision came down, Lacy was "out" for the third time.

"Since Lacy left second base of his own volition and should have been aware of the possibility of Moreno receiving a base on balls and since there was no rules misinterpretation by the umpires, the protest is disallowed," said Feeney.

Tanner had argued, logically enough, that "a mistake should be rectified in any business."

"THERE AIN'T NO RULE"

But as every schoolboy knows, baseball is a sport—the National Pastime. It's not a business at all.

Although pitchers collect game balls as souvenirs of their sterling mound performances, what really gets them impassioned are their rare displays of prowess at the plate.

Imagine Whitlow Wyatt's delight the afternoon of July 3, 1942, when he creamed a pitch from the Phillies' Frank Hoerst and sent the baseball flying toward the left-field seats at Shibe Park. Consider the Brooklyn Dodger pitcher's chagrin moments later when he was called out at second base.

Wyatt was no Pete Reiser on the base paths, but he wasn't that slow: He had been victimized by two umpires' conflicting calls.

His drive, leading off the fifth inning, had landed in the lower deck so far as Umpire Tom Dunn was concerned. As Wyatt headed toward second base, Dunn gave the homer signal. The pitcher then slowed down and went into a glorious home-run trot. But the ball was suddenly headed toward the infield. It had bounced back onto the outfield grass and was relayed by Ernie Koy, the left fielder, to Albie Glossop, the Philadelphia second baseman. Glossop put the tag on a nonchalant Wyatt. Another umpire, Ziggy Sears, called Wyatt out. The way Sears saw it, the ball had bounced off the screen atop the fence and so remained in play.

What Should Wyatt Have Been Credited With?

It quickly became very crowded in Sears's vicinity: Brooklyn ballplayers surrounded him, arguing that Wyatt had been thrown out only because Dunn had lulled him into a trot by ruling his drive a homer.

Bill Stewart, the home-plate umpire, figured the Dodgers had a point, but the rule book was no help here. It didn't envision this sort of mix-up. The umps finally decided that the baseball had not, in fact, gone into the seats. But it hardly seemed fair to erase Wyatt from the bases. So Stewart called it a double, figuring that Wyatt would have made it to second if Dunn's eyes hadn't deceived him.

Now it was the Phillies' turn to scream. Manager Hans Lobert insisted that Wyatt be called out, and when he couldn't convince the umps otherwise, he played the rest of the game under protest.

Stewart soon came under even more ferocious attack—from the stands. The turnout that afternoon was an underwhelming 1,646. By time the fifth inning ended, it had dwindled to 1,645. A fan seated behind the Dodger dugout hurled a pop bottle at the ump. It fell short and shattered, but at Stewart's order, the spectator left the scene in the grasp of a policeman. (Hoerst, the Phillie pitcher, also departed about that time as the Dodgers built a 4–0 lead in the inning.)

"THERE AIN'T NO RULE"

When the game ended as an 8–1 Brooklyn victory, the Phils' protest was filed with the National League. It would be denied: Since there was no rule to govern the case, the rule of fairness would apply.

Five years later, the same type of snafu arose, and once again the Dodgers were in the middle of it.

With St. Louis leading Brooklyn, 2–0, in the ninth inning of a game at Ebbets Field on July 20, 1947, the Cardinals' Ron Northey drove the ball deep to center field. As Northey rounded second base, Beans Reardon, the umpire at third, signaled home run. So Northey slowed down. But then the ball caromed back. Seeing the baseball apparently in play, Northey picked up speed again and headed home, only to arrive a split second after Eddie Stanky's relay to catcher Bruce Edwards. Umpire Jocko Conlan called Northey out.

Both Conlan and Larry Goetz, the other umpire on the bases, disagreed with Reardon's home-run call. They saw the ball strike a railing atop the fence, and the majority view prevailed.

Northey would have had an inside-the-park homer if Reardon hadn't deceived him momentarily. But the umpires refused to reverse the "out" call.

YOU BE THE UMPIRE!

Should the Umps' Confusion Cost Northey a Homer?

The Cardinals paid the price of the umpiring mess when the Dodgers scored three runs in the bottom of the ninth for a 3–2 victory. So Cardinal Manager Eddie Dyer protested to the league office.

National League President Ford Frick upheld the protest, awarded Northey a belated homer and ruled that the game was a 3–3 tie that must be replayed in its entirety.

Recalling how another umpiring crew had unraveled a similar dispute back in 1942, Frick leveled a rare blast at his umps.

"Just why . . . the three umpires failed to meet with an application of common sense and fairness a situation which obviously was the fault of their own actions is a matter this office is unable to understand," he groused.

So in both the 1942 and '47 disputes, the rule of fairness prevailed. The Brooklyn Dodgers won the first argument but lost the second one. Which, in view of the circumstances, certainly seems fair.

Bill Doran will never be remembered as a home-run hitter. But one Saturday night in August 1991, the Cincinnati Reds' infielder hit a drive into the right-field seats at Riverfront Stadium that would truly be memorable.

"THERE AIN'T NO RULE"

Doran's shot didn't decide a game, but it did set off a bitter dispute that wound up in federal court: It was the $5 million swing.

The Reds were trailing the Giants, 7–3, in the eighth inning when Doran hit a ball that landed close to the foul pole in right. Dutch Rennert, the first-base umpire, called it a home run. But when a swarm of Giant players charged after him, Rennert decided they might be right. Their protests seemed too impassioned to be brushed off.

What Should Rennert Have Done?

The rule book tells umpires that if they're sure they called a play correctly, they shouldn't be "stampeded by players' appeals to 'ask the other man.' "

But if an umpire isn't certain, he's supposed to seek help.

That's just what Rennert did, and when the screaming was over with, it was another umpire who took the heat.

Rennert went to Gary Darling, the home-plate ump, and asked how things looked from his angle. Darling's call: "Foul ball." And that's the ruling that stuck—Doran would have to swing again.

Now it was the Reds' turn to swarm in fury.

Cincinnati Manager Lou Piniella—a man with a formidable temper—put on a marvelous show. For starters he threw his hat at Darling's feet, prompting the ump to throw him out. Then he ran to home plate, kicking up some dust and scooping fistfuls of dirt.

YOU BE THE UMPIRE!

"He was so mad, he couldn't talk," Giant catcher Terry Kennedy remarked afterward. "He was squeaking like a mouse."

Then Paul O'Neill, the Reds' right fielder, threw a Gatorade cooler onto the field, earning the right to join Piniella in the clubhouse.

Now the Saturday night crowd of 46,969 joined in the fun, trashing the field.

"It looked like a ticker-tape parade out there," said Giant outfielder Kevin Mitchell. "You didn't know what would come out of the stands next—ovens, iceboxes. It looked kind of beautiful at first."

Finally, the crowd quieted down and Doran went to the plate again, this time drawing a walk from the Giants' Francisco Oliveras.

That was only Round 1 for Piniella. The Reds lost the game, and the next day he had some choice remarks.

"I honestly feel Darling has a bias against us and won't give us a call all year," Piniella was quoted as saying in *The Cincinnati Enquirer.* "We've had more complaints against him than any other umpire. He comes to Cincinnati and doesn't make the calls right, and we're tired of it."

But Darling wasn't the only ump who thought Rennert was wrong. Doug Harvey, the crew chief, who was umpiring at third base, said afterward that he, too, saw the ball curve foul. Harvey reported that Doug Hallion, the second-base umpire, also viewed it as a long strike.

Piniella was fined a thousand dollars for his outburst by Bill White, the National League president, and three days after the incident, he apologized, saying, "I overreacted in anger and frustration."

But the stakes would now get immensely higher. The same day Piniella said he was sorry, the Major League Umpires Association and Darling filed a $5 million defamation suit against the manager, charging that he had "severely damaged" the "sterling reputation" of Darling and all the other umpires.

Four months later, a settlement was reached.

The terms weren't revealed, but Piniella now seemed the umps' best friend.

"The major league umpires are, in my opinion, the finest officials in any sport today," Piniella said in a statement issued through the commissioner's office when the settlement was announced. "Under difficult circumstances, they acquit themselves with the very highest degree of professionalism and this has earned the respect and esteem of everyone in the game.

"I have high regard for Gary Darling's integrity and deeply regret comments that may have maligned his character in any way."

Lovely language that could make a lawsuit go away.

Back in the 1930s arguments weren't settled in quite that manner. One afternoon, Umpire George Magerkurth had it out with the Cubs' Billy Jurges over a home–run call. The issue was similar to that in the Piniella-Darling dispute but the method of combat was very different: Magerkurth and Jurges engaged in a spitting duel.

Except for creation of the designated hitter, baseball's rules haven't changed radically between the thirties and the nineties. But there has certainly been a switch in weapons when it comes to the game's eternal bickering: The well-aimed stream of tobacco juice has given way to a high-powered stream of legal motions.

Has baseball progressed?

The answer won't be found in the rule book.

Sources

Newspapers

Some baseball tales seem too good to be true. So I've looked to on-the-spot accounts. The following papers helped in separating fact from fiction: The *Atlanta Constitution, Baltimore Sun, Boston Herald, Brooklyn Eagle, Chicago Tribune, Cincinnati Enquirer, Detroit News, Los Angeles Times, New York Times, Philadelphia Inquirer, St. Louis Post-Dispatch, San Francisco Examiner, Seattle Times* and *Washington Post.*

YOU BE THE UMPIRE!

Baseball Publications

Baseball America, Baseball Digest, the *Baseball Guide,* the *Baseball Research Journal,* the *Sporting News* and *USA Today Baseball Weekly.* In citing current rules I referred to *Official Baseball Rules,* 1991 edition, published by *The Sporting News.*

Books

Bilovsky, Frank, and Rich Westcott. *The Phillies Encyclopedia.* New York: Leisure Press, 1984.

Durocher, Leo, with Ed Linn. *Nice Guys Finish Last.* New York: Simon & Schuster, 1975.

Einstein, Charles, ed. *The Fireside Book of Baseball: Fourth Edition.* New York: Simon & Schuster, 1987.

Fleming, G. H. *The Unforgettable Season.* New York: Holt, Rinehart and Winston, 1981.

Garagiola, Joe. *It's Anybody's Ballgame.* Chicago: Contemporary Books, 1988.

Gerlach, Larry. *The Men in Blue: Conversations with Umpires.* New York: The Viking Press, 1980.

Goldstein, Richard. *Spartan Seasons: How Baseball Survived the Second World War.* New York: Macmillan, 1980.

———. *Superstars and Screwballs: 100 Years of Brooklyn Baseball.* New York: Dutton, 1991.

Gutman, Dan. *It Ain't Cheatin' If You Don't Get Caught.* New York: Penguin Books, 1990.

SOURCES

Kaplan, Jim. *Playing the Field*. Chapel Hill, N.C.: Algonquin Books, 1987.

Lowry, Philip J. *Green Cathedrals*. Cooperstown, N.Y.: Society for American Baseball Research, 1986.

Marazzi, Rich. *The Rules and Lore of Baseball*. New York: Stein and Day, 1980.

Musial, Stan, as told to Bob Broeg. *Stan Musial: The Man's Own Story*. Garden City, N.Y.: Doubleday & Co., 1964.

Peterson, Harold. *The Man Who Invented Baseball*. New York: Charles Scribner's Sons, 1969.

Peterson, Robert. *Only the Ball Was White*. Englewood Cliffs, N.J.: Prentice-Hall, 1970.

Ritter, Lawrence S. *The Glory of Their Times*. New York: Macmillan, 1966.

Seymour, Harold. *Baseball: The Early Years*. New York: Oxford University Press, 1960.

Thorn, John, ed. *The Armchair Book of Baseball*. New York: Charles Scribner's Sons, 1985.

Thorn, John, and Pete Palmer, eds. *Total Baseball*. New York: Warner Books, 1989.

Tiemann, Robert L., and Mark Rucker. *Nineteenth Century Stars*. Society for American Baseball Research, 1989.

Veeck, Bill, with Ed Linn. *Veeck as in Wreck*. New York: G. P. Putnam's Sons, 1962.

Voigt, David Quentin. *American Baseball: From Gentleman's Sport to the Commissioner System*. Norman, Okla.: University of Oklahoma Press, 1966.

YOU BE THE UMPIRE!

Waggoner, Glen; Kathleen Moloney; Hugh Howard. *Baseball by the Rules.* Dallas: Taylor Publishing Company, 1987.

Wallop, Douglass. *Baseball: An Informal History.* New York: W. W. Norton, 1969.

Magazine Articles

Borst, Bill. "Did Charlie Hughes Really Manage the Browns?" *Baseball Research Journal* [Society for American Baseball Research], 1991.

Eldred, Rich. "Umpiring in the 1890's." *Baseball Research Journal,* 1989.

Gonzalez, Raymond J. "Protested Games Cause of Muddled Records." *Baseball Research Journal,* 1985.

Hersch, Hank. "It Was Touch and Go." *Sports Illustrated,* October 21, 1991.

Kermisch, Al. "Bat, Almost Six Feet Long, Used in N.L. Game." *Baseball Research Journal,* 1989.

Klem, William J., with William Slocum. "Umpire Bill Klem's Own Story." *Colliers,* March 31, April 7, 14, 21, 1951.

"Reading, Writing and Rhubarb." *Time,* May 6, 1957.

"Something on the Ball." *Newsweek,* August 16, 1965.

Summers, Bill, with Tim Cohane. "Baseball Boors I Have Known." *Look,* July 5, 1960.

SOURCES

Thornley, Stew. "Millers Topped Minors in Odd Protests." *Baseball Research Journal,* 1984.

Wind, Herbert Warren. "How an Umpire Gets That Way." *The Saturday Evening Post,* August 8, 1953.

Wulf, Steve. "A Squawk About Balks." *Sports Illustrated,* May 2, 1988.

Wulf, Steve, and Jim Kaplan. "Glove Story." *Sports Illustrated,* May 7, 1990.